APPALACHIAN
REVIEW

VOL. 48, NO. 4
FALL 2020

TRADITION. DIVERSITY. CHANGE.

EDITOR
Jason Kyle Howard

BOOK REVIEWS EDITOR
Emily Masters

STUDENT ASSISTANTS
Skylar Bensheimer & Christopher Stuchell

MANUSCRIPT READERS
Katherine Scott Crawford & Patti Frye Meredith

ESTABLISHED IN 1973
PUBLISHED QUARTERLY
by Berea College
CPO 2166
205 N. Main Street
Berea, Kentucky 40404
www.appalachianreview.net

The short stories in this publication are works of fiction. Names, characters, places, and incidents are either the products of the authors' imaginations or are used fictitiously. Any resemblance to actual events, locales, or persons, living or dead, is entirely coincidental. The views expressed in the creative nonfiction herein are solely those of the authors.

Electronic submissions only at www.appalachianreview.net

Distributed through a partnership between the University of North Carolina Press and Duke University Press. Basic subscription price: $30/year for individuals, $60/year for institutions. For subscription requests and inquiries, visit the magazine's website, email subscriptions@dukeupress.edu, or call 888-651-0122 (toll-free in the US and Canada) or 919-688-5134.

CONTENTS

BOOK REVIEWS

CONTRIBUTORS

COVER PHOTOGRAPH

House Show by Mallory Cash

EDITOR'S NOTE

JASON KYLE HOWARD

Layoffs and loneliness, the feeling that the world, dark and cold, is closing in. These themes form the backdrop of Merle Haggard's "If We Make It Through December," a masterpiece of American songwriting about a literal and figurative winter. It's a song I have known all my life, one of those so embedded in memory and family history that I cannot remember *not* knowing it. And this winter, I am finding some solace in Haggard's lyrics and in the weariness of his craggy voice.

Hard times, these are, what with the number of Covid-19 cases and deaths skyrocketing, with millions out of work, with our politics growing increasingly malevolent and outright dangerous. Our current moment is as chilly as "the falling snow" that Haggard describes, but instead of turning to the arts for escapism, I have caught myself seeking out music, literature, and film that confronts the rough and rocky parts of life. Much of the writing in this issue of *Appalachian Review* has consequently taken on these themes, beginning with the work of this year's featured author, Wiley Cash.

Since he strode on to the literary scene in 2012 with his debut *A Land More Kind than Home*, Cash has been celebrated as a voice of the Southern working-class, one that deepened with his follow-up *This Dark Road to Mercy* and his most recent novel *The Last Ballad*, a *New York Times* bestseller. And now, we are proud to introduce you to "A Great Distance," Cash's new short story, in which he conjures a memorable character and place, as well as an interview in which he discusses his working-class roots and how he wants to see "the South survive and thrive" by confronting its moral failings.

In a special feature, Sylvia Bailey Shurbutt contributes an essay exploring Cash's devotion to his home region and how, in *The Last Ballad*, he tells the story of Ella May Wiggins, a small-town mill worker who makes a fateful choice to fight for workers' rights and social justice in the Loray Mill Strike in 1929. Now, nearly a hundred years later, poet and essayist Victoria C. Flanagan confronts the haunted landscape of the strike—how the place has "flipped to high-class lofts" as the strike's history and meaning have been "shoveled over."

This issue also features "Socks and Junior," a moving essay from Denise Giardina on how she, her mother, and a pair of cats all grew up in their own ways in a West Virginia coal camp; "For What It's Worth," a powerful story from Jayne Moore Waldrop, which will appear in her forthcoming linked story collection *Drowned Town*; and poems by Waldrop, Marc Harshman, Barbara Costas-Biggs, Jamey Temple, Amy McCleese Nichols, and Cynthia Alby.

As we creep further into the woods of this dim winter, my prayer is that you might find some warmth and identification in this issue. May Haggard's words soon become a reality for us all: "Everything's gonna be alright, I know." ■

A GREAT
DISTANCE

WILEY CASH

When she was six years old, she spent two nights lost in the woods. Her mother and father had decided to camp in the Smoky Mountains for the weekend, leaving Raleigh on a June morning and arriving at the park entrance in mid-afternoon, just in time to unpack the car at the campground, pitch the tent, and get a fire going before nightfall.

On Saturday morning the girl and her parents hiked to the top of Mt. Le Conte where fog wrapped the summit in a gauzy fabric so dense the girl couldn't see beyond the crags and red spruce that marked the place where the ground fell away into white nothingness.

That evening, her father buried stuffed green peppers wrapped in cellophane beneath the coals of the fire while her mother made tea by heating water on the camp-stove. When her parents' backs were turned, the girl slipped off to the edge of the campground. She was always doing this: crawling to the center of the circular clothing racks at the mall; climbing onto shelves in the grocery store to hide behind stacked boxes of cereal.

She hid, not really hiding from anything, and she waited, not really waiting for anything either.

Dusk had settled by the time she decided to walk back to her parents' campsite. She expected to cross the paved road that led to the parking lot, but she stumbled upon a stream instead. She stood by the babbling water and looked for the trail because she knew it led back to the campsite, but it was difficult to see too far into the woods, so she decided to turn around and head back the way she'd come.

She found the paved road easily enough, but she couldn't decide which way led to the parking lot and which way to the campground. She turned left, and after walking for a few minutes she was certain she heard voices and saw flickers of light through the trees, so she left the road and soon found herself at the creek again. When she turned around the road was gone.

That night she slept beneath an enormous shrub whose twisted branches had woven themselves into a low canopy of green leaves and large white blooms. She fell asleep listening to the creek roiling over the rocks. She woke often during the night, disturbed by what felt like the light touch of a hand on her back, the whisper of a voice around her head. In the morning she found the shrub's soft, white blooms sprinkled all around her.

The next day dawned cloudy and gray, and the light that reached the forest floor was barely enough to distinguish day from early morning or dusk. She slept often, and when she woke she wondered if she were dreaming, and she wondered if it were in her dreams that she heard someone's voice and felt their presence.

■ ■ ■

A park ranger found her sitting beneath a stand of old growth hemlocks just after dark on her third day in the woods. In the yellow beam of the flashlight, his young face appeared clean and kind, and he introduced himself before telling her of how many people had been looking for her.

"Where's the woman?" she asked.

"What woman?"

"The woman that was here."

"Let's find your parents," he said.

The girl was not surprised that her mother wept while holding her, her hand combing over the back of the girl's head as if brushing the experience away from her memory. Nor was she surprised to find that her father's usual moodiness had given way to a quiet joy that was anchored in the overwhelming sadness and fear that he had weathered since the moment she had gone missing.

After being interviewed by park authorities at a ranger station, she and her parents left early the next morning and drove home to Raleigh. Her father hardly spoke while he drove. He wore the same clothes that he'd worn since the night she went missing.

The girl's mother sat in the backseat and held her in her arms, occasionally choking back a sob.

"It's all right, baby," her mother said. She moved the girl's hair out of her face and used her thumbs to wipe her tears. "You're safe now." She wrapped her arms around her again. "I know it must have been scary to be all alone."

"But I wasn't alone," she said. "There was somebody there." This felt true, but even as she said it, she did not know if it was.

■ ■ ■

Although Raleigh was the state's capital, word of mouth moves quickly when carried by death or pain or mystery. Much was made of the girl's time in the woods. She only gave one interview to the local newspaper before her parents decided that she was too young for so much attention, especially because she insisted on telling the story of someone being with her in the woods.

On nights when she couldn't sleep, her mind's eye would follow her path through the woods, stopping first at the spot where she'd hidden from her parents, then moving along the trail to the stream and the paved road before stepping into the darkness.

As the years passed, the girl could not help but feel that her parents' lives had continued without her while she was lost and that she would always be three days and two nights behind them. In this way they became and always remained strangers to her.

On nights when she couldn't sleep, her mind's eye would follow her path through the woods, stopping first at the spot where she'd hidden from her parents, then moving along the trail to the stream and the paved road before stepping into the darkness. By the time she lay down beneath the white blooms and twisted branches her eyes would've grown heavy and she would feel herself slipping off to sleep, and she would wait for someone or something, but she didn't know who or what it could be.

During college, when she shared her bed with her boyfriend, she would tell him about the things she'd heard and felt in the woods. Over the years, she'd learned the names of the things she'd felt and heard at night: the damp feet of salamanders that scurried along her skin; the mysterious hoot of an owl she was never able to spot; the snort of a deer. She shared these things at night, starting with her college boyfriend and continuing through all of her relationships that followed. As she had whispered beside these boys she would listen to their breathing slow, the mattress giving as their bodies surrendered to sleep, her voice fading away to silence before she found herself alone in the woods. Eventually, all of these boys became one boy, their faces blending to a shadowy composite in the dark of a bedroom.

"I bet you were scared," the boy would say.

"I don't think I was," she would say.

"But you were out there in the woods. At night. Alone."

"I don't think I was alone."

"Of course you were."

■ ■ ■

For her, time was a marble rolling back and forth around the basin of the Great Smoky Mountains, unable to breach the rim of the hills in order to roll free.

■ ■ ■

She left Durham after work on a Friday afternoon in early summer, and by dusk she had checked in to a hotel in Gatlinburg just outside the park. The next morning, she arrived at the park's western entrance and crept along in a long line of cars and SUVs full of parents and grandparents and children. There were very few people on foot, and she saw no one resembling the campers she and her parents had been. She parked and grabbed her water bottle and tightened the laces of the boots she'd bought online and set off on the paved road that led from the parking lot. The campground was still there, and she thought she could estimate the exact spot where her father's old tent had sat, the peak embarrassingly sealed with silver duct tape, her mother on her knees trying to light the stove, her father's back to them both while he poked at the fire.

The Mt. Le Conte trail was there as well, and something about this surprised her, as if trails and old-growth trees and centuries-old boulders were things that could've been moved and resettled over the intermittent years. She followed the trail, and at every sign of water she stopped and tried to decide if this could be where she'd become lost, if this could be where she'd mistakenly stepped off into the woods. She spent the day this way, going up and down the trail, looking for spots along the creek that seemed familiar, several times going all the way back to the campground before setting out again.

By late afternoon she was out of water, tired, and hungry, and her new boots had carved blisters into her heels. As she walked back to her car she wondered whether or not she should return in the morning to try again. At the edge of the parking lot she passed a ranger's station and decided to stop for a map that she could open across the bed in her hotel room that evening.

The building was warm and stuffy inside. She stood before a bank of pamphlets that advertised local attractions. From the counter behind her, a man's voice asked if she needed help.

When she turned she discovered that the voice belonged to the ranger who had found her all those years ago, his face now deeply lined and his eyebrows and temples graying. She asked if he remembered her; he smiled and apologized that he didn't. She told him who she was and how they'd come to meet, and she understood that perhaps he was one of the only people she'd ever really known.

The ranger locked the door and took off his hat and left it on the counter. She followed him to the office where he handed her a cup of coffee and got a cup for himself. He offered her a seat and he sat down at an old metal desk. It all came back to her: the worn carpet, the yellow-ochre walls, the topographical maps, the smell of coffee, her mother's arms tight around her while her father answered questions.

The ranger told her he'd found seventeen children who'd been lost in the park over the years, but she'd been the first. He was twenty-five when he found her sitting in the darkness beneath the hemlocks.

"What was I doing when you found me?" she asked.

"You were sitting there like you'd been waiting," he said.

"Did I seem scared?"

"No," he said.

"Did I mention anyone being with me?"

The ranger looked down at his coffee.

"Yes," he said. "A lot of kids who are lost see things too."

It embarrassed her, and she confessed that she was able to recall very little about her time in the woods and that she'd spent the day looking for the places she remembered. He stood and went to the map on the wall and used the eraser-end of a pencil to show her the ranger's station, and she followed the eraser as it skidded across the map to the campsite. And then he moved the eraser to the spot where he'd found her. It seemed like a great distance.

"Would you be able to find it?" she asked.

He studied the map for a moment.

"Yes," he said.

"Can you take me there?"

"Tomorrow," he said. "Come back tomorrow. It'll be too dark soon."

The ranger picked his way through a ring of keys and locked the station. The sky had settled to a deep purple. By the time they walked to the parking lot the darkness had begun to close around them like a warm blanket.

They stopped at her car and she fished through her backpack until she found her keys. The parking lot had emptied.

The sky had settled to a deep purple. By the time they walked to the parking lot the darkness had begun to close around them like a warm blanket.

"I'll come back tomorrow," she said. She opened her car door and sat down.

"Okay," the ranger said. "Look for me at the station."

"And you'll take me?"

"Yes," he said.

They told one another good night, and she sat and watched him walk back toward the ranger's station where his truck was parked. After he disappeared she started her car and drove a loop back to the campsite where she parked and then stepped into the woods.

She did her best to picture the map in the office. The light had faded almost completely, and the forest rose up in the dark shapes of trees. Once it became difficult to see the ground before her she pulled out her cell phone and used its flashlight to pick her way toward the distant spot she had fixed in her mind.

To her surprise, she found the hemlock stand easily enough, and she stopped at a particular tree and tilted her phone's light toward the tree's trunk, following it until the light reached the ground.

This was where he had found her.

She turned off her phone and sat down at the base of the tree. She looked up into the darkness and spotted the stars beyond the hemlocks' boughs. Her eyes adjusted slowly, and soon she was able to see the forest around her, and then she heard the babble of the stream not twenty yards away.

She turned on the flashlight again and splashed across the stream, the light catching the glowing eyes of the fishing spiders hiding along the bank.

She hadn't walked far when she found the same rhododendron where she'd spent those two nights almost twenty-five years earlier. It had grown considerably, and it was weighed down with the same heavy white blooms. At the base of the tree lay a young girl, her back turned, her body curved in sleep. She turned off her phone's flashlight, and as her eyes adjusted to take in the girl's sleeping figure, she felt something heavy and final close inside her with a near silent click.

The little girl's dark hair lay splayed over the side of her face, and she considered reaching out and moving it off her cheek and out of her eyes, but instead she sat down beside her, placed her palm on the girl's back, felt her body rise and fall in its breathing. The girl stirred.

She lay down beside the girl, positioned her body around the arch of the girl's back. She listened to the girl's quiet breathing, the nearly inaudible rustle of animals and insects moving over the earth, the voice of the water running not far away. She fell asleep.

She did not know how much of the night had passed when she heard the one sound she was not accustomed to hearing: the sound of something heavy moving in the woods nearby, and then the sound of it crossing the stream toward her. She sat up and saw the beam of a flashlight playing through the woods. He called to her. She lay down again beside the sleeping girl and listened as the ranger's footfalls drew closer. She closed her eyes as tightly as she could, as if doing so would keep out the approaching light. Despite all she couldn't remember and everything she would never be able to recall, she knew one thing for certain: They were not yet ready to be found. ■

AN *APPALACHIAN REVIEW*
CONVERSATION

WILEY CASH

This autumn, in between virtual readings, interviews, and Zoom conferences with book clubs across the country, bestselling novelist Wiley Cash was completing final edits on his much-anticipated fourth novel. Set in 1983 in eastern North Carolina—a departure from his previous books, which are all rooted in the state's western mountains—*When Ghosts Come Home* centers on a sheriff facing a series of crises and mysteries amidst a challenging campaign for reelection. Winston Barnes, the fictional sheriff, is a haunted man, an adjective that might also be used to describe Cash himself.

The South—its landscape, its characters, the beauties and failings of its culture—continues to hold Cash captive. In a recent interview conducted over email, he characterized his writing as an attempt to "reclaim and investigate" his experiences in the region; he spoke about the influence of Southern writers including Ernest J. Gaines, Lee Smith, and Thomas Wolfe; and how he is seeking to give encourage other writers.

■ ■ ■

JASON KYLE HOWARD: From the outset, with *A Land More Kind than Home*, you established yourself as a true writer of place. Is that something that works more organically for you, or is sense of place something you consciously set out to do?

WILEY CASH: It was very conscious at first. I was living outside of North Carolina for the first time in my life, and I was deeply homesick. The early drafts of the novel were written in Lafayette, Louisiana, and the later drafts were written and revised while I lived in the Northern Panhandle of West Virginia. The familiar felt very far away, and in writing about western North Carolina, I was able to write about a place that I missed, a place where I longed to be. I was also plumbing the depths of my own experience as a kid —evangelical religion, rural life, family dynamics—so all of it was an attempt to reclaim and investigate.

Later, perhaps deeper in the writing of that first novel and certainly in the writing of my others, I saw my writing about

Wiley Cash

place as being both conscious and unconscious. So much of what writers do is unconscious, and reflecting a place that you know well certainly falls under that description. But I've always written about places that I love and places that I still hold dear, so during the writing I always consciously investigate and interrogate those places, both physically—meaning I return there to immerse myself—and spiritually and intellectually—meaning I do my best to ask hard questions about how to accurately recall, conjure, and portray these places on the page.

JKH: You are obviously very proud to be a Southerner, yet you never hesitate to critique the region for its failings. How do you strike that balance?

WC: When you love a person or a place, you want that person to be healthy. I want the South to be healthy. My criticisms are not mean-spirited. I want the South to survive and thrive, and it won't happen if we're always humping our toxic past around with us. I'd rather we unpack it, call it what it is, address it and repair it, and move on with a lighter load.

JKH: Why is writing about rural, working-class people so important to you?

WC: I come from rural, working-class people, and the older I get the more I understand how that has come to bear on my own life. My mother and father's people were all farmers turned mill workers from western North Carolina and the upstate of South Carolina. These people struggled from the farms to the mills to the suburbs. I was born in the suburbs, but I always felt anchored in the past. I especially feel that way now because I fully understand that it was the grit and determination of the old people that delivered me into the quality of life that I now have. I didn't come from money, and I don't have money waiting for me after some long lost relative dies. So—even though I'm sitting at a desk instead of tilling a field or tending to spinners in a mill—I feel a sense of what my ancestors felt; I'm hacking away at a job, always looking toward the next one, hoping that one will be the one that promises some financial stability.

JKH: The New York literary world can be provincial, but it is also often populated with people from all of the country who want to promote diverse voices. As someone with a major New York publisher, have you had experience with both sides of that world?

WC: To be honest, there have been times in my professional life when I've felt like the token Southerner. During my first editors' lunch in New York City, my publisher held it at Southern Hospitality BBQ, which was Justin Timberlake's restaurant. I understood then that we were playing into a certain kitschiness, but I didn't see it as anything but playful, never mean-spirited or judgmental. But there have been times when my hackles have been raised by things that have been said by other writers or artists from outside the region. Once, at a prestigious artists' residency, I told one of my tablemates that I was living in West Virginia. My tablemate lived in New York, and he went on to tell a lengthy story of the time he drove through West Virginia and witnessed what he described as instance after instance of shocking poverty. I told him that I had just left New York, where I witnessed instance after instance of people eating out of trashcans in the wealthiest city in the nation. I told him that I had never seen anyone eat from a trashcan in West Virginia.

JKH: You have become a real ambassador for other writers, especially voices who are often overlooked, with your creation of the Open Canon Book Club, The Land More Kind Appalachian Artist Residency, and other initiatives. Tell us a bit about that work.

WC: Unfortunately, the artists' residency has been paused due to Covid but it is an incredible opportunity brought about by some of our dearest friends in West Virginia. They own a farm where I used to farm-sit for them in a hayloft that had been converted to an apartment. I wrote and revised a lot of my first two novels there over the years. They opened a bed and breakfast on the farm a few years ago, and they brought up the idea of hosting artists and writers in the loft for two weeks a year. That's how the residency got started. It was really their generosity that brought it about.

I started Open Canon in the summer of 2018, and I did it after visiting countless book clubs that seemed to be reading books only by writers who looked like me. The book clubs always asked me to recommend books to them, and I found that they had not yet read many of the authors I would recommend. I thought, If these book clubs will take my recommendations, perhaps other people will as well. I figured out how to set up a sign-up form and an email newsletter, and after only a few days the Open Canon Book Club had thousands of members from around the world. I partnered with dozens and dozens of independent bookstores around the nation who were willing to offer discounts to book club members, and, sometimes, ship books for free. It happened quickly, and we haven't looked back. The goal of the book club is to introduce readers to the diversity of the American experience. I believe it's meeting that mission.

JKH: How does a writer promote others and maintain generosity without it consuming your own writing time?

WC: One thing that makes this easy and pleasurable is the fact that I know a lot of booksellers, so I find out about new books and debut authors earlier than the general public. I also get to meet a lot of authors at festivals and readings and conferences, so I'm always discovering people whose work I love. I read constantly, and I reach out to writers I admire, regardless of whether or not it's their first book—which was the case with Ashleigh Bryant Phillips's story collection *Sleepovers*—or their latest—which was the case with Lily King's *Writers and Lovers*. Those were two of my favorites this year.

JKH: You don't shy away from writing outside your own race, class, or genre. How do you approach that, and how do you respond to those who think a novelist should only write from their own lived experience?

WC: I think writers should write what they know and also what they're willing to find out. I come from a complicated region, and I can't only tell the story of straight, white men and tell an honest story about this place. And when stories feel real and urgent to me—which was the case with *The Last Ballad* —I can't wait for someone else who may check all the gender, racial, regional boxes to write them. So, I do my honest [best] to find out what I don't know, and then I open myself to the criticisms of my attempt. That is really all I know to do. My advice would be to do the deepest dives you can when writing outside of your own experience and culture, and then do the best and most honest work you can to represent that experience.

JKH: You've spoken a lot about the influence and inspiration of Ernest J. Gaines and Lee Smith on your writing and life. Who are other writers—or even books—that have most influenced you?

WC: There are several books that have inspired me, either with their style or scope or familiarity. They are *Look Homeward, Angel* by Thomas Wolfe; *Cane* by Jean Toomer; *Song of Solomon* by Toni Morrison; *Charming Billy* by Alice McDermott; and *Of Love and Dust* by Ernest J. Gaines. I am always thinking about or actively rereading one of these books. Of all of them, Gaines is my literary forefather. His work—on a craft level—has affected my own work more than anyone else's. But I am inspired by the scope of Wolfe's vision, the precision of Toomer's prose, the generosity of McDermott's writing, and the ways in which Toni Morrison's literary vision lies on an historical continuum.

JKH: You never hold back from sharing your political opinions. Do you think an artist has a responsibility to speak up on issues they care about, particularly in difficult times such as these?

WC: I can only speak for myself, but I don't see any separation between my role as a citizen and my work as a writer. ◼

WILEY CASH
AND THE TIES
THAT BIND

SYLVIA BAILEY SHURBUTT

As one reads the stories of Wiley Cash and looks at his evolution as a writer over the past decade, a singular characteristic overshadows all the other excellent qualities of Cash's writing: that is, his devotion to place, the quality that has most shaped him as a writer. In a *Bookbrowse* interview with Lisa Guidarini, Cash said this about the prominence of place in his writing: "I think place is probably the strongest aspect of my writing, at least I hope it is anyway. When I wrote *A Land More Kind Than Home*, I was trying to recreate western North Carolina because I missed it so much. I was living in southwest Louisana, and I found myself homesick for those mountains, seasons, and fresh water." Cash continues, "When I wrote the novel, I got to go back there."[1] Cash's three Gastonia novels—*A Land More Kind than Home, This Dark Road to Mercy,* and *The Last Ballad*—are all singular efforts of superb storytelling which brings to life a corner of western North Carolina, a part of Appalachia and the South well worth the knowing.

Wiley Cash grew up in the Piedmont area of southern Appalachia, in Gastonia which was famous as a mill town and the center of the textile mill culture of the early twentieth century. It was the setting for the 1929 Loray Mill strike, and singularly important in propelling that segment of the labor movement to the national spotlight. Many of the mill workers were sharecroppers or failed farmers who provided a cheap work force during and after the first World War, a time when the Piedmont area of Southern Appalachia come into economic prominence. Today Crowder Mountain looms within the confines of Gastonia's city limits, not far from famed Kings Mountain. The historical prominence and natural beauty of the region captured the imagination of Wiley Cash, who comes from a long line of Appalachian storytellers, which is to say, as Cash clarifies: "I come from a long line of liars."[2]

Cash's grandfather Harry Eugene Wiggins, from a South Carolina mill town called Enoree, was one of the earliest

1   Lisa Guidarini, "Interview with Wiley Cash," *BookBrowse*, 25 September 2015, https://www.bookbrowse.com/author_interviews/full/index.cfm/author_number/2153/wiley-cash.
2   Wiley Cash, "Meet the Author," in *This Dark Road to Mercy* (New York: William Morrow, 2014), 2-3.

storytellers or "liars" in Cash's family. Cash shares the story of his grandfather's telling his older sister that elves lived in a bush at the side of their house, and if she were quiet and patient she might get a glimpse some cool summer evening. Cash recalls his sister "sitting for hours by that bush, waiting for those elves to come out…She's still regarded as the best-behaved of the three of us." When Cash left the area in 2003 to attend the University of Louisiana at Lafayette to complete his PhD in English and creative writing, he had the good fortune to study with Ernest Gaines, the university's writer-in-residence.

Gaines showed him that his stories were "placeless," that they could have been written about anywhere in the country, in the world for that matter, and they achieved no evocation of place. Cash found that living in Cajun country was "strange and foreign," so he re-read *Look Homeward, Angel* and just about everything else he could get his hands on that featured home and mountains, and the words allowed him to visualize place: "I couldn't go to the top of Beaucatcher Mountain and look down through October leaves to see the city of Asheville at sunset. But, when I opened the pages of *Look Homeward, Angel*, I could."

Cash talked about his quest for place and home with his teacher Gaines, who shared his own story of leaving the plantation west of Baton Rouge, where his parents were sharecroppers, and moving to California to go to school and grow up away from Jim Crow—always with the rural South present in his mind, however. Gaines too found that when he read about home, it became suddenly real, visible, audible, and a place to write about and allow his characters to live and experience as he remembered it.[3]

Once when Cash and several classmates visited Gaines at his homeplace, they were walking and passed an old cemetery.

Gaines pointed out to Cash a grave marker and told him, "You remember Snookum from *A Gathering of Old Men*? He's buried right over there."[4] After that weekend as Cash was driving back to the university, across Louisiana's endless flat land in the fading light of dusk, he found that when he squinted his eyes and stared at the cloud bank on the horizon, he could almost see the mountains near Asheville. At that moment in time, he conjured a story for an image in his mind of a little boy smothered in a church healing, and *A Land More Kind than Home* was begun.

Both *A Land More Kind than Home* and *This Dark Road to Mercy* have become national bestsellers, with the former receiving a nomination for the Weatherford Award in Fiction and the latter an *O Magazine* Top Ten recognition. Both books are set in Gastonia, North Carolina, and both are contemporary and timely, with *A Land More Kind than Home* about a civic and church leader without a moral center. Both evince the remarkable talent of Cash, influenced as he is by such writers as Toni Morrison, Russell Banks, Charles W. Chesnutt, Kaye Gibbons, Flannery O'Connor, and Bobbie Ann Mason. Both stories are told though varied narrators, as this is the way storytelling and truth are revealed. Cash told Lisa Guidarini how important the voices of his characters are to him—their speech, dialect—but significant as well is the typically Southern style of storytelling: "Rarely are these stories told in a linear fashion; very often the storytelling is circular or digressive." He points to the example of Kaye Gibbons's *Ellen Foster*, "and the way Ellen, as the novel's narrator, moves chronologically with long stream-of-

---

3   Wiley Cash, "Why I Write about North Carolina," in *A Land More Kind Than Home* (New York: William Morrow, 2012), 5-8.
4   Guidarini.

consciousness digressions. The novel reads as if Ellen is telling the reader her story as it comes to her."[5]

While these two contemporary Gastonia stories have brought Wiley Cash into the national spotlight, it is his latest book, *The Last Ballad*, published in October 2017, that uses place to define the story of a person who literally trod upon this planet in an attempt to make it a better place, for her children, her African American neighbors, and her fellow mill workers. Ella May Wiggins gave her life for the union struggle to help mill workers during the 1920s. Place propels this story, but the novel takes on almost epic proportions as Cash attempts to tell a story that shaped the American social and historical landscape. Ron Rash captures the significance of Ella May Wiggins's life in his series of mill worker voices that constitute the *Eureka Mill* collection:

> *It was the fourteenth of September*
> *in nineteen hundred and twenty nine,*
> *when she made her last stand in a cottonfield*
> *a few miles from the South Caroline line.*
> *We won't forget the day*
> *strikebreakers struck poor Ella [May] down.*
>
> *They shot her in the chest and let her die,*
> *then took her body into town.*
> *she was just a linthead on this earth*
> *but in heaven she'll wear a crown.*
> *We won't forget the day*
> *Strikebreakers struck poor Ella [May] down.*
>
> *Oh mothers tell your children this sad tale*
> *so they will tell their children when they're grown.*
> *She sacrificed her life to save the union.*

Eureka workers, she was one of your own.
So don't forget the day
strikebreakers struck poor Ella [May] down.[6]

Cash humanizes this epic class struggle for workers' rights by telling the tale through a range of characters' perceptions: Ella's, her children's, her African American union colleague Hampton Haywood, a mill owner and his family (Richard, Katherine, and Claire McAdam), and through the perception of white civic leaders in Gastonia who wish to seize the narrative or story of the Loray Mill strike in order to tell an "alternative truth" that better suits the racist and classist status quo that dominated North Carolina in 1929 when the strike took place. For example, the narrator quotes from the *Gaston Transom-Times* which

Cash understands that he who controls the language, that he who determines the narrative, can write the "truth" as he sees fit...

seeks to portray the strike as a Bolshevik plot to overturn the racial system, even to advocate something as "dreadful" as "full racial, political and social equality for the negro race."[7]

Cash understands that he who controls the language, that he who determines the narrative, can write the "truth" as he sees fit, illustrating the historical significance of the "power of storytelling." Even Lilly, Ella May's daughter, laments the tenuousness of truth as she talks about the expensive stone monument that the AFL-CIO put up for her mother: "They spelled her last name incorrectly, Mae instead of May, which

5   Ibid.
6   Ron Rash. *Eureka Mill* (Spartanburg: Hub City Writers Project, 1998), 38.
7   Wiley Cash. *The Last Ballad* (New York: Harper Collins, 2017), 218.

is ironic considering how much money they spent and how important they said she was to them."[8]

Ella May's chief importance in the union's struggle for workers' rights was for the purpose of controlling the narrative, as hers was an appealing story, told with both music as well as words. Union leader Beal calls the game precisely for what it is when he tells Ella, "Word's out about you, Miss May." Ella responds, "What word?" Beal replies, "You made quite the impression last night… with the story you told and your song. It all made quite the impression on Loray, on the newspapers too."[9] Later Beal tells Ella, "You could become the face of this strike, Miss May. Loray's already scared of you. Your story, your music… You could be what turns the tide of these people."[10]

A false narrative or story was what the mill owners used to seduce tenant farmers and poor laborers to leave their farms for the company mill towns that promised an economic panacea: "The piedmont mill barkers who stood atop stumps in the lumber camps and in knee-deep mud on the tenant farms had promised safe, sanitary housing in mill villages. Children would be educated at mill-sponsored schools. Souls saved at mill-sponsored churches. Paychecks cashed for scrip at mill-owned stores."[11] The truth, however, was subsistence living, endless debt, wages that no family could live on, and back-breaking work under intolerable conditions, six days a week, twelve hours a day. While the profits at mills like Loray "exploded" during and after the war because of the close proximity to cotton markets, rail transportation, and a cheap labor supply, what the mill workers found when they took these jobs and moved to the company town were "filth and disease and the kind of poverty they couldn't get away from once it took hold of them."

This scenario was certainly the case at American Mill No. 2 in Bessemer City, where Ella May and her African American neighbors in Stumptown lived and worked. When the Council of Concerned Citizens of Gaston County and the upstanding mill owners of Gastonia eventually break the strike, they make no excuses for their violence, because theirs is a cause that resonates among the majority of the white citizens of North Carolina, certainly among those power brokers who rule the mills and civil government—their mantra being: "We need to take our city back."[12]

Cash begins his story of the Loray Mill strike with Ella May as a single mother struggling to feed and care for her family, her husband John Wiggins having left, saying he "wouldn't live among niggers anymore" or work for nothing in the Bessemer mill. Ella is reprimanded for missing her shift one night when she has to remain home to care for her three-year-old daughter Rose, sick with whooping cough—having already lost her son Willie to the disease. When her supervisor Dobbins ignores her request to be put on a day shift so that she can be with her children at night, she is called into the mill owner's office. Confronted with missing her shift because of her sick child, Ella is told by mill owner Goldberg's brother: "What if all my employees had sick children, Mrs. May? What about me? What if I had a sick child at home and decided that I couldn't come to work? Who'd run this mill?" Ella sees the futility of trying to elicit any empathy from the mill owner, and he tells her, "But I can assure you of this …: it'll be much easier to find someone to operate your spinner than it will be to find someone to run this mill. I expect you'll keep that in mind next time you find yourself with the desire to stay home."[13]

8   Ibid., 59.
9   Ibid., 119.
10   Ibid., 121.
11   Ibid., 96.
12   Ibid., 196.
13   Ibid., 18, 19.

Ella knows that she must do something, and ironically she muses: "She didn't think for a minute that Goldberg's brother or Dobbins or anybody else at American would ever murder her, but she knew for certain that working there might kill her just the same." In desperation she attends the workers' rally at the Loray mill, the largest and most modern mill in North Carolina. And there she meets Sophia who wants to use Ella to organize the African Americans at the Bessemer mill. Ella speaks and sings, and the power of her presence and her voice escapes no one, including herself. When faced with not being able to return to her mill job having associated herself with the strikers, she begins a new job as union organizer and feels that destiny has found her: "She knew she belonged here in

Ella speaks and sings, and the power of her presence and her voice escapes no one, including herself.

the midst of this shared experience, not just the rally but her whole life and all the poor men and women and children who had passed through it."[14]

Because all stories have such a variety of points of view and because truth is never found solely in a single narrative, Cash allows all the players to have a voice in telling Ella May's story. Some of the most poignant voices are from the wealthy McAdam family: the McAdam mill owner Richard, who has attempted to run his mill more humane by providing workers with brick homes and tolerable working conditions; Richard's wife Katherine, who befriends Ella, identifies with her loss of a child, and attempts to offer her both monetary and tangible support during the strike; and their daughter Claire, whose engagement to Paul Lytle, son of a wealthy southern planter, causes some discomfort among the more liberal McAdam family and brings home the truth about Claire's own family business. Claire's friend Donna points out the connection between the mill workers and Paul's poor tenant farmers who have replaced the slave labor of the old South. Claire objects, saying, "I told you, Donna, my father [is]…not like that. He treats his people better than that." Donna replies, "Are you even listening to yourself?…You talk about your father's employees as if he owns them…And you and your parents live in the big house that looks down on the rest of the family, … just like on Paul's parents' plantation. I bet they viewed their slaves as family too."[15]

Though Claire challenges her friend's characterization of both her fiancé's family and her own, she is troubled, and, like her mother, fears the role they will have to play in this struggle which the strike has brought to bear in Gaston County. At her engagement party, her father Richard is approached by the Loray superintendent, Hugo Guyon, with a request to support the Council of Concerned Citizens of Gaston County, "a small committee," Richard is told, "dedicated to ridding this county of the Bolsheviks and getting our lives and the lives of our people back in order." The "civic" group that constitutes the council—that is, mill owners, thugs, Pinkerton detectives, and southern rednecks—will indeed bring a violent end to the strike. Richard tells Hugo Guyon that he will give a donation and will see about providing the men that Guyon has requested in order to "let the Reds know they're outnumbered." He also listens with interest as Guyon tells him about Ella May, who "works at American in Bessemer City… trying to organize them there."[16]

---

14   Ibid., 13, 109.
15   Ibid., 158-59.
16   Ibid., 196, 198, 199.

Guyon and Epps determine to "kill a snake...lop off its head," if it threatens their way of life or the status quo; and Richard answers, "A snake with its head cut off can still bite you."[17] So the line in the sand is drawn, and a somewhat more than passive consent is provided by Richard and those moderates like him that allow prejudice and persecution to prevail. And Yeats's words from "The Second Coming" ring true in Cash's portrayal of this epic labor struggle—that in times of change or great social upheaval "the best lack all conviction, while the worst / Are full of passionate intensity."[18]

Another fascinating voice who tells Ella's story is that of Hampton Haywood, an African American union organizer who comes from New York to help Ella organize the Black Bessemer mill workers. Hampton has spent most of his life in New York, has been a Pullman Porter, and carries the scars of American racism. Cash begins the chapter which Hampton, whose father is killed by the KKK, narrates: "His father had shot and killed a white man in Mississippi in 1910."[19] No further details would be needed for the reader to understand the trauma that Hampton endured as a six-year-old watching his father being dragged away and brutally murdered after he tried to protect his home by committing the unthinkable for a Black man at that time.

On the night that the strike goes awry and violence and racism run rampant on the roads of Gaston County, Ella saves Hampton, calling on both Katherine and Richard for help— Richard prodded to action by the conscience of his wife. When the night of June 8th is over, the Chief of Police Aderholt is dead, warrants are out for the union leaders Beal, Sophia, and Ella, and events are set into play that will make September 14, 1929, one of those moments in history that signals another American tragedy. Ella's daughter Lilly has the last word among the voices that Cash provides to tell the story of Ella

May Wiggins and the Loray strikers, and Cash leaves us with something to ponder about historic truth and the truth of our individual lives: "There is an old saying that every story, even your own, is either happy or sad depending on where you stop telling it. I believe I'll stop telling this one here."[20]

Wiley Cash is doubtless one of the rising stars in Appalachian and American literature. He is a storyteller—a "liar"—who has discovered what Ron Rash, Robert Morgan, and many of the most talented Appalachian writers have found true: that by focusing on one place, a story can be told that is both specific and universal at once. ■

17   Ibid., 201.
18   William Butler Yeats. "The Second Coming." Poetry Foundation. 6 October 2020. https://www.poetryfoundation.org/poems/43290/the-second-coming.
19   Cash, *The Last Ballad*, 250.
20   Ibid., 372.

ARIA FOR LORAY MILL

Gastonia's Loray Mill strike of 1929 was one of the most notable labor strikes in United States history. In the strike's aftermath, seventy-one strikers were arrested. Eight strikers and another eight members of the National Textiles Workers Union were indicted for the murder of police chief Orville Aderholt. On September 14, a truck carrying twenty-two strikers was chased down and fired upon. One female striker, Ella May Wiggins, was killed. Though the strike failed to result in better working conditions and wages, the strike's controversy gave the labor movement significant momentum, propelling its national development.

I.

This is all simulacra. Strikers gone almost a century,
Loray Mill flipped to high-class lofts, factory muck
    and truck beds loaded with bodies—all of it

shoveled over. I know this place forgets.
Down Beaty, Preacher Bailey eyes the newspaper
    waiting on the drive. A request, maybe:

Forgive us. These are the things I'm made of: idling
red-and-rusted 250, the Capps mare put up
    and a fire lit, exhale of a midnight flatbed

headed for the state line. Long gone, I dream
of my home church's stained glass, the overlook
    where I'd watch planes take off and land—miraculous as ever.

A demand if I could beg it: Take me as I appear
to be, let me leave this place behind—

But I get an email:
someone's razed up luxury—bought that shuttered testament

and suddenly it's Loray Mill Village, script font shouting
a move-in special: *$99 deposit!* Already
they can't fill the place.

Shoppes, wine bar, *events hall,*
an *on-site history center*. I wonder: is it there
they list the thousand surnames

marked by a walkout? Memory's arbitration
laid bare, what of the 1,800 workers
who wouldn't bend to cut hours, stretch-outs—

families evicted by foremen despite the gleaming
Easter parade, the festive lights strung up the spires
in the name of the Lord and two days off?

I imagine Charlotte commuters clicking into an elevator,
shadow of a suit reflected in new steel—Are there photos,
in the polished lobby, of the marching National Guard? Snapshots

from the organizers' march on night shift? I imagine
the decorators have gilded, re-framed the police raid
on the strikers' tent city, violence disguised as charm.

This town could use some heroes, now and then.

One dead chief, sixteen men indicted for murder—*Life
revolved around the mill*, the site croons.
    Families worked together and knew one another personally.

These days we claim only what serves us: *skylights,
premium countertops, tanning center.* Opulence poised
    like a threat. The real math of '29:

    ten percent of my hometown on strike.

Did the sixteen or the seventy-one arrested
in a single day *know one another personally*
    before they were hauled off?

Were the families I know forged in cells?
Stop me if you know—when the judge declared a mistrial,
    labor leader's truck chased down, did Ella Mae see the bullet coming?

Headed east, Bessemer City to Gastonia, did she hum
as her blood stained the bench seat? Did she pray swiftly
    for her unborn son?

How many men does it take to kill
cruelty? How many men
    'til I know?

II.

Call it a curse, call it inevitable. I, too, forget
    my grandfather and his father and his father's father
ran production lines and watched from a mile away—

down Marietta and just off McArver—porch a refuge,
        pulpit, rally point. Same porch of my long Saturdays
picking, putting up, chasing the youngest kids in torment.

My great-grandmother thinking none of us wise
        to her stash and habit, post-industry
houses wilting down the block.

Daughter of such unspoken names, I go home these days only
        to bury, remember what the land allows: down here
we chain our dogs to a lead, let them run bare patches

in rye grass. Girls grow up waiting for the grip
        of a man's hand on the throat—we learn one hit
isn't the same as a beating. We jump, ritually,

from Buster Boyd Bridge to Lake Wylie below, trusting
        the water's deep, that we've not lost track
of seasons or drought—jump

and come up laughing, water January-cold.
        We smoked milds behind mulch fields,
drifted among shopping centers sprawled like burdock,

pretended not to notice as years passed, high school kids
        nodding out on the greenway. We skimmed
through youth. Lighter's click and sizzle

in bathroom stalls. A rusted brand
        of pride: freshly fifteen, I woke next to a cold body. Sixteen,
I dipped into the back of a drawer to get out of bed.

Inevitable, it felt like *what else?*
      I spat jargon—*skag, boy, bare, slam,*
raw, smack, dope—but called it the burden of this place,

some ghost-moan in pills' rattle, a turning away,
the steady refrain: *surely not my child.*
      Is it a wonder

that I say my name like an apology? All these stories
      I cannot tell in one place. Every mile north a fleeing
of my anonymous body, dope-sick and dumped

in an ambulance bay. Every mile back a duty, a debt:
      who, if anyone, can be saved?
I do the only thing I know—dedicate to names

I know well, speak lowcountry rites:

    Alex, Corinne, and Petey and Ashleigh

    and CM and Chad-O, Mike, Becca, Jess, Big Ray, AJ, RJ,

    JR, for the mother of the child starving next door.

      Let me remember and outrun.

    For Angel, Jordan, Drew, Anna, Hannah, Parker,

    Nat, and Jon.   For Spits and Hughes and Rachel, Liza, Dom.

    For Dom and Alex, always—I will remember,

I will arrive when called back, days carving
        wide highways, and learn a freshman drowned
under the bridge last May, the depth—

like all else—deceptive. Ruled an accident, and so many
        of us know better.

These are the things I am made of—we say nothing
        out of fear.
I go back home and old friends drop in, reminisce—

how could any of us know
        what to make of it? Mercy is a blade,
a dopplered yell.   All the while a trash pile smolders,

a hound barks once, and my cell phone waits
        there—in the pale kitchen—
with all the old possibilities. An anticipation,

an inevitability, maybe. A squib load
poised on the foreman's desk.

VICTORIA C. FLANAGAN

FOR WHAT IT'S
WORTH

JAYNE MOORE WALDROP

O ccasionally someone would stop Elmer Newby in a store and ask him why in the world he'd help the government run people off their land. Elmer always clenched his teeth and stiffened his shoulders. His cheeks turned red. "Hell, I didn't decide this. That was some fool in Washington," he told them. Elmer hated that folks had no choice about leaving, but he had to make a living. Every morning as he headed out to appraise property, he reminded himself that he had a family to support. A job to do.

Elmer started his real estate appraisal business after he returned from the war in Europe and attended college on the GI Bill. In the early years he struggled to keep the business afloat. He got his real estate license and sold a few houses when the bank account grew lean, but he preferred appraising land to showing houses. He was good with numbers. Coming up with the fair market value on a piece of property required figuring parcel size, square footage of structures, and finding the value of comparable tracts. Comparables were crucial to the calculation. The goal was to be as objective as possible because, in Elmer's mind and according to the standards of his profession, objectivity led to fairness for both the buyer and the seller.

During one long stretch without much work, Elmer decided he might need to close his business and take a job with a weekly paycheck. He knew Judy worried about the rent and whether they could afford things for the kids. He could get a route selling life insurance policies for Joe Flynn's agency or selling clothing for the suit factory. About the time he was ready to call it quits, he heard talk about another federal dam project, this time on the Cumberland River. The dam and the resulting massive reservoir required the government's acquisition of thousands of acres. Each parcel would be appraised to determine fair market value and a purchase price. Elmer felt like he'd struck gold.

His business took off. He appraised all sorts of property—houses, businesses, schools, tilled farmland—most of which would be under water or along the new higher shoreline when the lake filled. Entire towns were taken through the power of eminent domain. People lost homes and farms that had been in their families for generations. Old-growth forests were leveled. The sight of a mountain-sized stack of downed trees had caused Elmer to grieve for days, but that was the way of progress, even if it hurt to see. When the dam was finished, Lake Barkley would fill and flood the land, forever altering the place. There would be no going back.

The Barkley Dam project changed Elmer, too. For the first time in his life, he had money. He hadn't inherited a copper from his people, but now he had money. He and Judy took the kids to Florida for a summer vacation. They built a modern ranch-style home with a brick façade, by far the best house he had ever lived in. Elmer wanted his children to have a better life than he had known growing up. His own father had a hard time holding a job—he was bad to drink—which meant the family moved often to find work. From one rental house to another, one school to the next, they kept moving, never calling any one place home. Elmer didn't want that for his kids. He wanted them to know where they belonged. When he and Judy built the house, he knew exactly how much it cost, each two-by-four and every window, even down to the price of a brick or a roof shingle, and he had earned every cent needed to build it.

But he grew anxious as the last few Barkley tracts were acquired. The appraisal work would dry up with the dam's completion. He thought his business was sufficiently established, but he hated the thought of losing everything he'd worked for.

■ ■ ■

"Did you see the paper?" Judy had said when the news broke a few years ago. She stood at the sink washing breakfast dishes, already dressed for work in a yellow sleeveless shift, her auburn hair combed, a hint of orange lipstick applied.

Two days a week Judy worked in the children's section of the Mayfield Public Library. Their three boys had caught the school bus a few minutes earlier.

"Not yet," Elmer said as he poured himself a cup of coffee. He leaned toward her and gave her a peck on the cheek, glimpsing the freckles on the back of her bare arms. He wanted to lean down and kiss them but he didn't. He splashed milk into his coffee, then dropped in two saccharin tablets and stirred until they dissolved. He wore a white shirt with a narrow black tie, and after he had his coffee, he would slip on a jacket grown shiny from pressing and head to his small second-floor office over the Ben Franklin on the courthouse square.

"There's big news," she teased.

He sat down at the table, picked up the *Sun-Messenger*, and read the headline: *Kennedy Administration Proposes New Recreation Area Between Lakes*. Elmer's heart raced as he read. The Tennessee Valley Authority proposed buying out every property owner on the narrow strip of land between the rivers —now lakes—to recreate a wilderness for hiking, boating, fishing, and other leisure activities. Three hundred miles of shoreline stretching from Kentucky into Tennessee. As many as 170,000 acres, 1,500 dwellings and farms to be appraised. The story quoted governors and congressional delegations from both states who were delighted with the news. So was Elmer Newby. The Land Between the Lakes project was a godsend, assuring steady income for years.

Judy's hands grazed the back of his neck. "So, what do you think?"

"That I'm the luckiest son of a gun that ever lived," Elmer said.

She laughed and squeezed his shoulders. "I'm glad you realize that," she said.

Elmer stood and turned to face her, putting his arms around her. He pulled her close. "I'm not taking anything for granted," he said, then left for the office. His mind shifted into high gear, making plans, deciding who to call at the local TVA office. Because of the Barkley work, he was on a first-name basis with several of the land acquisition superintendents. It might be years before actual appraisals began—federal projects were notoriously slow and cumbersome—but Elmer wanted to be the first guy in line.

His wait for the work to begin went on and on. A few months after the LBL announcement, President Kennedy was shot and killed in Dallas. Then the feds argued over whether the land should become a national park or a recreation area. They argued with the people over how many acres would be acquired and whether commercial development would be allowed. The people fought to keep their property, now destined to become a tourist attraction. Some residents wanted to develop their own resorts on the lakes. President

Every person Elmer dealt with was as mad as hell, regardless of their circumstances.

Johnson stepped in, insisting that landowners needed more time to protest and let their voices be heard. The people got their hopes up.

When the acquisitions finally commenced, the government took it all. The protests had changed nothing. TVA claimed every tract in the forty-mile peninsula that straddled the Kentucky-Tennessee line. Nobody wanted to leave their homes. Some claimed the government was stealing their land with low-ball offers for now-lakefront property. Every person Elmer dealt with was as mad as hell, regardless of their circumstances. Nice homes and rusty trailers, owners rich and poor, Black and white, young families and old widows. A few times Elmer believed he'd not survive the work. "Don't get out of that car" became a common greeting when Elmer arrived on an assignment.

A farmer named Adams was particularly convincing. Elmer had driven more than an hour to reach Cravens Creek, a remote area where every other homeowner had been bought out for Barkley. Only Adams remained. His house sat at the end of a long road—more dirt than gravel—that few traveled these days. As Elmer parked and reached for the door handle, he spotted a man with a headful of white hair waiting near the corner of a log corncrib. Adams was ready for him, perhaps alerted by the rooster tail of dust thrown up behind Elmer's car as he approached.

"Stay where you are," Adams said. Elmer saw that the man held a shotgun. From his years in the war, Elmer recognized its shape as a Winchester Model 12. The Perfect Repeater. His heart raced.

"Sir, my name is—" Elmer stopped as he saw Adams lift and shoulder the shotgun, preparing to draw a bead on him. Elmer raised his hands shoulder high. "I'm not armed, Mr. Adams, and I don't want any trouble," he said.

"Get off my land and we won't have any trouble," Adams said.

"I'm just trying to do my job, sir, but this can wait," Elmer said. "I'm getting back in the car now." He eased back into the driver's seat and drove off. When he checked the rear-view mirror, Elmer saw that the old man had not moved or relaxed. He remained in a fighting stance, ready to follow through. Elmer drove on. From that day forward, he kept a loaded snub-nose Smith & Wesson in the glove box. His children understood to never turn the latch when they rode in his car.

Despite his efforts to grab as much work as he could, some jobs stayed with him. Some nights he laid awake, remembering Donnie and Evelyn Richards being forced to leave. Unlike most of these assignments, he knew Donnie and Evelyn. They were Judy's distant cousins. Evelyn's eyes were the kind of green that only rivers possessed and she had looked deep into his own. "Where will we go, Elmer?" she had said, refusing to blink. "We've never lived anywhere else. This is our home." The fact that she had spoken so tenderly to him had struck him harder than if she had shouted or cursed.

The clock ticked beside his bed as he wondered who came up with an idea that exiled them all and why it had ever been approved, but when morning came Elmer went back to getting the work done, keeping his family of six fed, and his business afloat.

One day he rose early to recalculate the Richards appraisal. He had kept it in a separate file and held back on submitting his final valuation, but he needed to turn it in. He needed to get paid for the job. On a fresh form, he reentered the same details —square footage, acreage, number of rooms—but he changed the home's condition from fair to excellent. When he got to the office, he'd find new comparables to justify the higher sale price.

At breakfast Judy had to say his name twice to get his attention when they had their coffee. "What is it, Elmer?" she asked, sliding her hand over his. "I can't stop thinking about Donnie and Evelyn," he told her. "It's pitiful," and then he found that he was choking on the rest of his words and she didn't press him further, tightening her grip on his hand. He finished his coffee and looked at her, noticing flecks of river-green in her eyes, too.

"Some of these folks will never get over this," he predicted.

■ ■ ■

The phone rang as Elmer unlocked the office door. He left the keys in the lock and scrambled to answer the call. It was

Clyde Edmonds, who ran the land acquisition office over at Golden Pond. Clyde handed out appraisal assignments.

"I've got a holdout over in Pleasant Grove. Old colored man won't talk to anybody. Already run off two other appraisers. We can't have any more bad publicity," he said. Elmer remembered the newspaper stories about Ada Chilton and the public outrage about what had happened to the old woman.

"You've got a bunch of amateurs working for you," Elmer said. "You need somebody who can get the job done."

"You want to try?"

"Have I ever let you down, Clydie?

"I'll up your fee by fifty dollars if you can get Nate McCracken's property appraised without any trouble."

"Sign me up," Elmer said. He could use a little extra money. School started in a few weeks, and his children looked like they had outgrown everything in the closets. Elmer liked a challenge. He also wanted to be Clydie's first choice whenever the agency needed an appraiser.

But Elmer worried. He hoped Nate McCracken wouldn't be another Ada Chilton, the old woman who had used her shotgun to blow out a windshield when another appraiser came to talk about buying her property. She, too, had been a holdout. Her land was the exact location proposed for the new dam. The Corps of Engineers wouldn't alter the plan because an old woman refused to sell. The situation turned ugly when somebody lured Miss Chilton into town on the pretense of a meeting. While she was away from home, government-hired crews moved in with bulldozers, leveling her still-occupied residence and then torching it. As fire engulfed all of Miss Chilton's worldly possessions, smoke was seen for miles like a signal of things gone wrong.

When Elmer heard about what happened to the old woman, he couldn't believe something like that could happen in America. He assured friends and family that he had nothing to do with Miss Chilton's file.

■ ■ ■

Before heading to Pleasant Grove for the day, Elmer filled a couple of mason jars with ice water, and packed two sandwiches and an apple to last him through the day. All the restaurants between the rivers had closed. A few small general stores with rough wood floors were still open if he needed a cold bottle of pop late in the day.

Elmer drove toward Gilbertsville where two lanes of U.S. 62 crossed the top of Kentucky Dam. Built in the 1940s, the dam was the first of the big local federal projects, designed for flood control and to generate hydroelectric power for rural western Kentucky. To the right of the narrow highway Elmer glimpsed Kentucky Lake beyond the low guardrail, its surface glistening in the morning sun. To the left, in between passing cars and powerlines that carried electricity generated by the dam's turbines, he saw the swirling currents of the Tennessee River below the gates. The lake was wide and calm; the river narrow and wild. As he gazed, he heard the honk of a horn. He looked back to the road and corrected his unintentional drift into oncoming traffic.

Two decades had passed since the first impoundment, but Elmer still viewed the lake with awe. Numbers churned in his head about the yards of concrete that went into the construction, the cost per yard, workers employed, gallons of water flowing per second. Even when he wasn't appraising, his mind automatically put a cost-benefit analysis to everything around him.

The lake itself was stunningly beautiful, the dam a technological wonder. Elmer never imagined a body of water so big, right here in his own backyard, like an ocean had been plopped down in the middle of the country or a sixth Great Lake had formed. He never dreamed of something like this so close to home. Elmer was from an adjoining landlocked county, a place more of soil than water that hadn't lost an acre or a dollar in tax revenues from the building of two dams, the resulting reservoirs, or Land Between the Lakes. In fact, he and his neighbors benefitted from the creation of thousands of jobs and cheap, plentiful electricity. It was progress, plain and simple.

Optimistic to his core, Elmer remained excited about what the lakes meant for western Kentucky, both for business and on a personal level. Nearly every dollar he had earned came from his own hard work, much of it connected to the federal projects. He was a self-made man. He liked progress and wanted to be part of it. A couple of summers ago, he had borrowed a musty surplus Army tent from a friend to take his

Elmer never imagined a body of water so big, right here in his own backyard, like an ocean had been plopped down in the middle of the country or a sixth Great Lake had formed.

family camping at the new Kentucky Dam Village State Park. Judy was six months pregnant with their fourth child.

"I'm not sleeping on the ground," she had said.

"You don't have to. I borrowed a cot for you," Elmer said.

"It's so hot, honey. My feet might pop if they swell any bigger."

"I bought one of those inflatable rafts for you. You can float in the water to stay cool."

Judy's scowl lifted a bit. "We don't have sleeping bags, either" she said.

"Roscoe let me borrow a couple. The boys and I can make a pallet with blankets. It'll be fun," he said. He put his arms around her. "I promise I'll do the work."

In a red metal Coca-Cola cooler, he packed hot dogs tinted a deep pinkish color, milk, lunchmeat, mustard and ketchup. The picnic basket was filled with potato chips, corn flakes, Little Debbie oatmeal cakes, thin-sliced Bunny Bread, hot dog buns, a large stack of paper plates, and tin mugs to use for drinks and as cereal bowls. He stashed a watermelon in one of the backseat floorboards. It rolled over the boys' feet when Elmer braked or took a curve too fast.

At the state park, they found a campsite at the lake's edge and Elmer tried to pitch the tent. Eventually he got it to stand by roping it to nearby trees.

"I think Roscoe forgot some of the tent poles," he said. "It should hold for the night, though."

For less than twenty-four hours at the lake, they swam, watched ski boats zip by, and fished from the bank with a borrowed pole they all shared. One of the boys caught his first, a small sunfish with vibrant orange markings. Around the campfire, they roasted two packages of hot dogs on straightened coat hangers and drank cold pop, something the kids didn't get at home. The children chased tiny toads until dark when they switched to catching lightning bugs. When they could run no more, they collapsed onto a pallet made from damp-smelling sleeping bags and blankets that nearly filled the tent. As his family slept, Elmer sat alone by the fire, watching the embers and looking at the stars. Water stroked the shore at a level the old river people never dreamed possible.

"If my luck holds out and the work keeps coming, I want to buy a lot or a cabin over here," he told Judy on the drive home the next day. "There's something about this place."

■ ■ ■

Pleasant Grove, a crossroads originally situated near a bend of the Cumberland River, had been settled around an iron furnace built in the 1800s by enslaved laborers. More recently the community had its own motel and restaurant, both listed in the Negro Travelers' Green Book. They'd already been torn down. A white frame Baptist church and a one-room school had been leveled and burned last month.

Elmer thought about the tract of land owned and occupied by the holdout, Nate McCracken. A title search at the Lyon County courthouse revealed that McCracken's family had owned the land for nearly a hundred years, the recorded deed dated shortly after the Civil War. Title had been passed from generation to generation of McCrackens. While Elmer was at the courthouse, he found several recent transfers of similar properties on which he could calculate his comparables.

As Elmer got farther from home, WNGO-AM faded to static. He spun the dial to find a closer station—WCBL in Benton—and heard the morning news, weather and livestock reports. The forecast was a hot one with a chance of rain in the late afternoon.

His dusty white Ford Fairlane rolled past razed farmhouses, dogtrot barns, and churches. He recalled the demolition work in preparation for the lakes where everything—buildings and trees—was cleared. This time was different. For LBL the forests, creeks and ponds were to be left untouched; only signs of human settlement and industry were doomed. The plan was to return the area to wilderness as if no one had ever lived there.

Elmer turned down a lane bordered by honey locusts twisted and knobby with age. A *Keep Out* sign had been nailed to the tree closest to the road. Elmer's heart rate started to climb, and his fingers tightened around the steering wheel.

He took his foot off the gas. Since the incident with old man Adams, he had changed the way he approached a property. His car crept up to the house, this one a neatly kept but unpainted frame structure sitting close to a large barn, also unpainted.

Elmer relaxed a bit when he saw a man working in a field between the barn and house. At least he knew he wouldn't be looking down the barrel of a shotgun right off the bat. Elmer took a deep breath as he parked the car and turned off the engine. He reminded himself that his work was backed up by the law. He had it in writing, a court order that gave TVA and its agents the right to trespass to accomplish a buyout. He kept a worn copy in the glove box, next to the pistol. He hoped he didn't have to reach for either.

He got out of the car and slammed the door. "Mr. McCracken?" he said in a loud voice as he walked toward the barn. The man's shovel slowed and he turned, standing beside the trench he was digging. He was a tall man, unstooped, and he wore work clothes, a faded checked dress shirt and bib overalls covered in dirt. His heavy boots were caked with dried mud. He didn't smile or wave or approach in welcome, but he leaned on his shovel as a big brindle dog of an unidentifiable breed came from under the porch, barking and loping toward Elmer. Its tail stayed in a curl over its back.

"Can't you see I'm busy?" the man said with a directness that surprised Elmer. Most Black men of a certain age in this part of the country still followed the well-known rules of engagement when addressing a white man, although Elmer had never set much store by that way of thinking. He decided he preferred Mr. McCracken's rude tone to looking down a shotgun barrel, and besides, his immediate concern was the approaching dog, now closer and starting to growl. He braced himself. "Can you call off your dog, sir?"

"Rufus! Get over here," McCracken hollered. The dog stopped, then turned and walked toward his owner.

"Thank you, sir. I see you're busy, but I need to talk to you. My name's Elmer Newby and I...."

"And you're from the government," the man interrupted.

"Not really. I'm from over at Mayfield, and I'm a real estate appraiser. I need to see your land so the TVA can make you a fair offer for your place."

"Don't have time today. Got to dig this ditch before the rain comes," McCracken said. He went back to digging.

"Well, sir, we're running out of time to give you a fair price. You've got a nice piece of ground and the government ought to pay you what it's worth. If I can't see your property, we might miscalculate," Elmer said.

"Not today," McCracken said. He kept digging. Elmer thought about his next move.

"How far you going to take that ditch?"

"Out to the road."

"That's going to take you the better part of a day."

"Reckon so. Don't have time to waste," McCracken said, pointing toward the sky.

Elmer thought hard. Why the man was digging a new ditch confounded him, knowing that the government would hold title soon. But the man said he needed the ditch dug before the rain began, and Elmer needed to finish the appraisal. Pulling out the court order wouldn't help accomplish either task.

"How about this? I'll help you dig your ditch, as long as it takes us to finish. And when we're done, you spend the same amount of time showing me around your place so I can finish my work," he said.

Elmer waited. In a moment, McCracken stopped digging. "There's another shovel in the barn," he said.

"Alright, sir. Let me get my boots from my car." Elmer walked back to his sedan, took off his coat and tie, and rolled up his sleeves. He exchanged his shoes for work boots and headed to the barn for the shovel.

They worked side by side for two hours. Neither said much, only questions and answers about the ditch. In that time, Elmer thought about the years McCracken had spent working this land, surely never imagining being forced off this late in life. He watched McCracken's efficient movements as he cut straight into the earth and sent wide arcs of dirt into the air. By midday, they finished the job. Both were covered in sweat and dirt. McCracken extended his right hand, and Elmer shook it.

"Come get a drink and wash up," McCracken said. He led Elmer around back of the house to a well where he drew up a bucket of fresh water. Elmer washed his hands and face, then

Elmer thought about the years McCracken had spent working this land, surely never imagining being forced off this late in life.

ran his wet fingers through his hair to slick it from his brow. He cupped his clean hands for a drink of the shockingly cold water coming from deep in the ground.

"You want a bite to eat?"

"Thank you, but I've got a sack lunch in the car. I'll sit here in the shade and eat if you don't mind." McCracken nodded and went inside. Rufus scooted under the porch.

Elmer got his food and sat on the edge of the steps, hoping for a breeze to help him cool off. He ate a bologna sandwich and listened to kitchen sounds from inside. A rattle of dishes and maybe a skillet. Then the screen door opened and McCracken reappeared. He carried a plate mounded with scrambled eggs and two pieces of light bread. He scraped half of the eggs into a tin pie pan on the porch and called his dog. Rufus leapt onto the porch and gulped his share. McCracken sat down in a straight-back chair to eat his meal.

"How long have you lived here, Mr. McCracken?"

"Name's Nate. Been here all my life. Born here. My daddy before me, too. Never lived any place else," he said.

"Must be hard to give it up."

"Never thought I'd ever have to." Nate's aged brown eyes looked straight into Elmer's younger blue ones. "We worked hard so nobody could take it away from us. Now I'm supposed to just hand it over," he said, shaking his head. "My great-granddaddy was born into slavery over in Christian County. And my great-grandmama's people worked the iron furnaces here between the rivers. Also slaves. They worked right alongside those Chinamen."

"Folks came all the way from China to work these furnaces?"

Nate nodded. "Paid 'em next to nothing and worked 'em to death. Worked 'em like slaves. They're buried right over by the old furnace. Never made it back home."

Elmer looked in the direction of the barn when he heard a riot of blue jays, squawking and diving toward a calico cat that walked toward the house. He turned back to Nate.

"You've always farmed?"

"All I know is farming and tending this place."

"Ever think about selling it?"

"Never, but we about lost it a couple of times. It's hard to hang on after a bad flood like '37. We'd have a flood once or twice a year. Or we'd have a drought, like in '52. Hard to pay the taxes when your crops don't make nothing," Nate said.

"How'd you manage?"

"We'd get work at another farm over in Hopkinsville or Paducah, getting in hay or setting tobacco. Sometimes my daddy got on with a road crew," he said. "We might not have much else, but we paid those taxes. As long as we owned this farm, we were free. And we wouldn't starve to death, either."

Elmer nodded. His throat tightened; he didn't say anything for a few minutes. His face grew hot as he thought about the damned fools who came up with this plan, who decided to take this tract and many others from the rightful owners. Those damned fools were the same ones who paid his fees. He sighed, feeling the weight of his own complicity in the plan but there was no going back. He thought about Nate's parents and grandparents, how they'd worked for generations to provide this home, a rightfulness in their title that derived from the good-faith exchange of taking care of the land then living from its bounty. Elmer had never experienced a long connection to one spot. He'd never known a homeplace, but he understood the desire to provide for a family. He carried it with him every day as he headed to work, and he wanted his numbers to reflect that common ground.

When he saw that Nate had finished his food, he stood up. "I need you to show me all the good parts of your property. Just the good. Don't show me anything bad or tell me about a leaky roof or a well about to go dry," he said.

Nate called for his dog then offered some advice. "You watch your step. We've got plenty of rattlesnakes and water moccasins since the lake came up. Guess they're looking for high ground, too," he said. "Rufus here is good at finding snakes before they find me."

For the next two hours, Elmer followed Nate across his cornfields, hayfields, and meadows blooming with cardinal flower and goldenrod, through woods thick with tulip poplars, oak and beech. They walked along gravel creek beds, ponds and former river bottom land that had become lakeside property. Elmer paid close attention as Nate explained his farm and his practices, details spoken with a quiet confidence that stemmed from years of working the same land. They stood on the shore and looked across the lake, its waves lapping against his fifty-five acres.

"When they built Barkley, did they pay you right for your river bottoms?"

"Not near enough. That was my best ground. It's been hard to make up for it," Nate said.

They stopped by a small, fenced cemetery with simple limestone markers. All the names began with M. "There's my mama and papa," he said, pointing where small bouquets of faded red plastic flowers were planted at the headstones. Grandparents and great-grandparents were nearby. Nate looked around the cemetery.

"It's just as well, I figure. I'm the end of the line. Got no children, no cousins, nobody to heir it anyway," he said.

Elmer's view of the property shifted, and he began to see the land through its owner's eyes, not as a collection of objective facts and figures. A few times he had shaved small corners by reconsidering one subjective assessment or another when a price didn't reflect true value. Evelyn Richards' river-green eyes and her soft, haunting voice had nudged him before. He looked at the McCracken house, its unpainted boards, wavy-glassed windows, each log in the old barn, and decided he had no measure of its worth. The generational labor that had built the place made his numbers feel thin, his own new house cheap by comparison.

It was late afternoon when Elmer walked toward his car to leave. The western sky had darkened.

"Looks like we got our work done just in time," he said, pointing to a line of clouds moving in. Nate eyed the storm and nodded. The men shook hands, and Elmer patted the dog's head. Before Elmer got in the car, he turned back.

"Where will you go, Nate?" he asked.

"Some of the neighbors plan to stay together. They've bought a piece of ground not far from that new town. Fairport. I guess I'll go with them," he said.

As Elmer drove off, the rain began to fall. He turned on the windshield wipers and thought about Nate McCracken having to pack up and leave a homeplace that had withstood floods, droughts, births, deaths, joy, hard times. A true home. Elmer started working the numbers in his head, wondering how he'd calculate a fair price. There were no comparables. ■

ONCE MORE HOME

Over the hill he sees
      a few more minutes sneak away
      under the cover of leaf-fall and
      turkey cackle and
      the first wood smoke of October.
He puts dates
      on his calendar, radiator fluid
      in his Ford 150, storm
      windows in the house, fodder
      in the shock, firewood
      in the shed.
He even puts words
      on his tongue
      to hold onto time: *anniversary,*
      Sunday School, market day,
      turn-the-clock-back day,
      Thanksgiving, Christmas,
      says aloud *remember, remember, remember . . .*
      but it's only *culling* and *harvest* linger.
In the graveyard
      on his mother's stone:
            but about that day or hour
            no one knows.
But who is it knows,
      not the hour, but the minute
      when the words began to slip
      not away but beyond
      the ability of his tongue
      to summon them once more home.

MARC HARSHMAN

YESTERDAY I ASKED MY SON

Do you see that there? The bee

stumbling into a flower, legs padded

with pollen, his hive-mate heavy-flying

to the clover of the neighbor's unmowed

yard. Yesterday, we saw a katydid on a high

electrical wire like a perfectly balanced

leaf. Yesterday, we could look at the sun,

right at it, behind the smoke rolling

in from the west, behind the almost-fall

river fog. You called it a blood moon,

correcting yourself after saying it, *No,*

that's the sun, and we were mesmerized,

perhaps cautious, knowing we shouldn't

look for too long. Yesterday I almost told

you that the world is mangled-up, that

sometimes, even for all the katydids balancing

on wires, it can be me that does the injuring.

BARBARA COSTAS-BIGGS

THE RELEASE

I am on the bank of the Pigeon River.

The woman upstream is fly-fishing.

I am trying to keep my smallish boys

in line, quiet, to not break

her concentration. I've never been a swimming

hole-type of woman, but this river has one,

swirls blue green in the sun

shards, almost lures me in past my ankles.

She casts and the lime green line floats close.

She casts and the line moves like a sound

wave, even whirrs before it splashes.

My Greek grandfather tied his own flies,

now lost to time and an estate sale.

I remember his back better than I remember

his face: flannel against the Michigan spring,

sitting at the end of his dock on Mona Lake.

I grabbed mussels from the shoreline, swatted

black flies, watched his large hands

bring the rod back, watched its arc, then

the release.   I lose myself

to the kingfisher across the river, watch

him and his orange chest hunt from above.

And then she does it, almost without me noticing:

brings in the fish, river trout,

pink-bellied, sleek as a bullet, slips it into her creel.

BARBARA COSTAS-BIGGS

AFTER DEATH: AN INVENTORY, BEGINNING WITH A DOG

with a line from Anne Sexton

The winter descends here, a few

yellow leaves hanging on. I am

walking down the street, our street,

with your dog. My dog now.

Small, a terrier, unlike the hunting dogs I

have always kept. She's wearing a coat.

This dog, I call her my imprinted

duckling. At my heels when I cook, at my hip

when I sit. She burrows under the down

of my blanket, and I wonder how

she breathes under there, her pushed-in nose

flush against the softness.

From your bedroom, from a mirrored tray

from the top of your dresser, I took

the half-full bottle of Chanel No 5,

slipped it into my purse, felt like a thief.

There's no way not to feel like this, like a vulture,

scavenging for the thing that will help

keep you in my memory.

Horsehead bookends. A tiny bust of Plato

I brought you from Greece. A pocket-

sized copy of *The Gift of the Magi.* Your pincushion.

The winter has descended, but the sycamore

disagrees, holds its crispy leaves tight.

I thought about your practicality, and took

a few perfectly folded bath towels. This morning

when I dried off, the dog sniffed at one, sat

at my feet, licked my ankles.

BARBARA COSTAS-BIGGS

CIRCA 1994

after Jason Isbell's "The Life You Choose"

It wasn't Jack and Coke, it was Southern Comfort in Taco
Bell cups full with ice, no doubt on our way to another
viewing of *Pulp Fiction* or to Hoover Reservoir to steam
windows and dream of big cities and rock stars and
riot girls and whatever else it was that made sense to a
seventeen-year-old girl whose heart was only half alive. I
was always reading *The Bell Jar*, listening for that old brag
of my heart but never trusting it, sure that whatever it told
me to do would be wrong.

Last night was my twenty-year high school reunion. I
skipped it, not even curious about how the faces I knew
all those years ago have aged, because it wouldn't be a
surprise. I know what they had for breakfast this morning,
thanks to the phone in my hip pocket that dings and dings
and keeps my Twitter feed current. I skipped it and got
drunk with people I don't know and told them all, "I'm
skipping my twenty-year reunion for this" as if that brag
was meaningful. It didn't make me feel younger.

This town I live in now doesn't leave much to the
imagination. Tucked in a valley, surrounded by rivers
and foothills, not even outlet malls to help me waste an
afternoon. I have a house that's too small. I have children
getting too big too quickly. I drive an hour to work.
On Friday mornings, if my timing is right, I can speed
alongside the Amtrak Cardinal and wish and wish and
wish and remember.

BARBARA COSTAS-BIGGS

PYRO

MARIE MANILLA

Not sure if I drove there or if I was dropped off, but somehow I found myself on your doorstep, Kerry, in Wayne County, my county's more rural cousin. You'd recently moved here from who-knows-where and lived with your mother. I don't think you had siblings. I don't remember a father. I remember the doughnuts. Your mother bought a dozen and we ate one after another until we were sick. "I always wished I was tall," your mother said to me. Neither you nor your mother cleared five feet. You had other endowments some boys in our class valued. Big boobs and a ready laugh that bordered on hysteria.

You took me to meet your boyfriend, if he indeed was. We met in his side yard where local kids had gathered. Cute girls and lanky boys. Mark was blond and beautiful. He didn't act like your boyfriend. Didn't hug you, or hand hold, or drape his arm around you. He looked directly into your eyes, though, with an intimate knowing. A conspiratorial caring. He offered Pepsi and lawn chairs. He offered the same to all the kids, including the girls who sidled up to him. The way you watched those girls whose laugher didn't border on hysteria. Mark didn't seem to intimately know them yet.

"Let's go for a hike," you abruptly said. "I have something to show you."

We left Mark encircled by those adoring girls and walked down the road to a path that led into the woods. Cool shade offered relief until we spilled into an overgrown clearing where an abandoned travel trailer sat. It was a 1950s round top, two-toned, kudzu tangled and moldy. You shouldered open the door, and a musty smell wafted out along with gnats. The kitchenet counter was overloaded with empty beer cans, spent bottles of Boone's Farm. I wondered if this was a party haven for local kids, or if the detritus was solely yours and Mark's.

You slid along the bench seat behind the cantilevered table that likely folded down into a bed. I eased in across from you, the seat's Naugahyde skin brittle and splitting; guts of wood wool stuffing spilled out like finely coiled straw. You pulled out your cigarettes and offered me one. Struck a match and held it to the tip. Only then did I see the amber burns marring the Formica tabletop. So many forgotten cigarettes left to smolder.

It was hot in the trailer. Airless. Dust floated through sun motes.

Your mouth moved, but you weren't listening to your words, or mine. Your inner eye was back at Mark's house, or maybe it was here during a past rendezvous with the table folded down and Mark touching you now that no one was watching.

Where ever you were it animated your hands. You pulled a string of coiled wood wool from a split in the seat and held the tip of your cigarette to it. It smoldered and quickly burned down like a sprig of incense. Tendrils of smoke wafted in the air along with the dust. You did another one, and another, and finally yanked out a handful of wood wool and held your cigarette to it.

"Kerry." Everything in that aluminum box looked flammable, including us.

You laughed at my alarm, not the hysterical laugh, but a pained one that touched a nerve. Still, you watched as the bundle ignited and burned until you dropped it on the table where it snuffed itself out. I thought the game was over, but you yanked out another wad.

"Kerry."

Finally, you pushed the tip of your cigarette down into the slit, laughed as gray smoke drifted up, followed by crackling flames. You slid out of your bench, and somehow I leapt over the table to try and put the fire out. I swatted and batted but it caught so fast, and suddenly bees flew out from inside the cushion and stung me, and you. Their irate buzzing as the flames shot higher and higher. You dove outside first and I tumbled after as noxious smoke spilled from the door, through cracks in the windows kudzu had pried open.

"What should we do?" I said. "Should we go get help?"

You didn't answer. Just watched dark smoke roil into the sky, enthralled.

A loud pop from inside the trailer and you grabbed my arm and yanked me back into the woods, but in a different direction. Branches and vines whipped our faces, and I scratched at the stings on my hands and arms. Skin splotchy from the flames.

I'm not sure what happened next, if we made it to your house, if we washed up and washed out the smell. I do remember the sirens, plus the charge in your eyes as you led me back to the clearing. All those kids from Mark's house stood around as fireman attended to the flames, though I have no idea how they got equipment to it, if there was equipment. If they put the fire out or just let it burn. It was an abandoned trailer, after all.

Mark edged over to you and leaned down to mutter, "Did you do that?" His eyes were as charged as yours.

Your head tipped back and your laughter mingled with the smoke.

■ ■ ■

Four years later I sat in another trailer, a mobile home not meant for traveling. It's where I lived while in college two-hundred miles north of Wayne County. The phone rang and it was Atlanta Police. The officer wanted to know if I'd seen you, heard from you, knew where you were.

"No." That was the truth. You and your mother had packed up and moved. Did you even graduate high school with us? "Did she run away?"

"I'm afraid I can't say," the officer said.

When I hung up I thought the worst. You were so young and big-city police were tracking you down. Did you commit a grander crime? Fall in with dangerous men who weren't charmed by your edge, your risky infatuation?

■ ■ ■

The lady who cuts my hair, Dreama, has a missing daughter she hasn't seen in twenty years. There's a coffee mug on Dreama's station printed with her daughter's face. Her image dangles from a charm around Dreama's neck.

Kerry, does your mother wear a tiny picture of you strapped around her throat? Light votive candles on your birthday? Or did you show up one night scared stiff and reborn? Finish college and marry and now live a fairytale life? I hope that's how it unspooled for you. But I Google you sometimes. No matches. No familiar faces or places and I inevitably go to the worst, a burning trailer in an overgrown clearing.

Kerry, did someone finally snuff you out? ■

EWE

The first ewe lamb was not born
She appeared
Unexpected
Exquisitely groomed
Each tight spiral of auburn fleece
As intricate as a watch spring

A Renaissance lamb
Eager to be depicted in oils
Adorning the neck of a shepherd
Fetching the wooly explorer from her wander
His tiny charge
Tuned to adventure
From the moment she materialized
Under her anxious mother's muzzle

CYNTHIA ALBY

ONE RARELY SEES

One rarely sees
A paean to the lymph nodes or liver
Or a sonnet for the
Nitrogen fixing bacteria.

Love and hate run roughshod
Over tender pancakes,
And what remains for coots and carburetors,
No. 2 pencils, multicolored butterbeans?

Poets do not often tend
To the pirouette of the ceiling fan
Or whatever it is that makes
Jelly gel.

Running water "tickles" over
Pebbles in a stream
But when it trickles from my faucet
Its burble merits not a couplet.

Songbirds sometimes earn a verse
Of course, or envy,
While slender spatulas, whisks
Remain unsung

When really
What is more lyrical than
Sturdy cotton socks
My toothbrush
Your inseam

CYNTHIA ALBY

STILL LIFE WITH FARM

I may as well lie down
As the pastures slip into their winter greys
Tin sky, sheep shrouded

CYNTHIA ALBY

SOCKS & JUNIOR

DENISE GIARDINA

I don't know where my mother found Socks. Given the number of strays in our poor coal mining county, with no animal shelter or animal control officers, I'm sure it was not difficult. One day kitten Socks just appeared. She was black with white feet, thus her name. I was thrilled. I was five years old and I had several dolls. But I never cared much for dolls with their stupid frozen faces and motionless limbs, nor was I interested in pretending to take care of a fake baby. Here was a real living toy to play with.

My mother had that *No Pets in the House* rule, brought over from her eastern Kentucky raising. My father's dog Candy had been forced upon her, but she would hold firm otherwise. She installed Socks on the back porch with a cardboard box and blanket and food and water bowls. But I was allowed to bring kitten Socks inside every afternoon for play, "until she grows up", my mom proclaimed. I proceeded to pull out my doll clothes and cram the kitten into them, to force her into my doll carriage and parade her around. When she tried to escape, I put the buggy's movable hood over her neck to try and hold her down. As she strangled, she scratched my hand to no avail because she was so small. So she did the only thing else she could think of—as soon as I let her go, she fled. Soon enough, she fled at the very sight of me.

I was crushed. Socks didn't want to play. Even worse, she didn't like me. I considered this, and then a light bulb came on inside my five year old brain. Socks did not like to play the way I did because she was different from me. Socks was a cat. And Socks didn't like me because she was afraid of me. She was afraid of me because I was hurting her.

I have since learned that five is the age when most of us learn to empathize with others. A three year old cannot do it; a five year old can. At that time, I felt I had discovered the greatest secret on earth. I had imagined myself into the mind of another being. If they were suffering, I could understand that. And if I wanted someone to like me, I had to be nice to them. This was especially true of animals, who could not speak to beg for kind treatment. When I learned as an adult that Descartes believed animals had no feelings, no more than any machine, I was grieved. Descartes, I thought, had never grown up with a kitten or puppy. He had missed a lesson on empathy when he was five.

I realized I had dug myself into a deep hole where Socks was concerned. I would have to win her back, and I would have to plan how to do that. One day I went outside and found her sleeping in her box. She didn't wake until I was upon her, and then she started and squirmed to escape. But I only held her briefly, stroked her head, and then let her go. She ran.

I repeated the experiment a number of times, always on the lookout to catch her sleeping. Her struggles to escape weakened. At last I ventured to pick her up and hold her against my chest, stroking her and whispering to her. Then I quickly let her go. Before long she let me hold her. She purred. I promised her I would never be mean to her again, never force her to wear dolls' clothes, or ride in the doll baby buggy. She was not a doll; she was an animal, with dignity. I didn't voice this last part; I didn't have such a vocabulary then. But I sensed it.

■ ■ ■

By age eleven, my father had become a family breadwinner. Although my grandfather worked in the mines, and took the oldest boys, Joe and Frank, with him, it wasn't enough to provide for the family. So my father, terrified of mining, pursued odd jobs. He then survived the Depression as a young adult. He was both proud and a bit resentful, I think, that his own children did not need to work. He'd had no special treats as a child, and he didn't think we deserved them. *Don't get above your raising,* he often said. He also felt obligated to provide for his parents in their old age. A source of contention in our house. My mother saw a significant part of my father's income going to his mother, not his children. And she, also from a deprived Depression childhood, wanted the world for us. For her, it was her children against their miserly father.

My father worked and saved every scrap of his income, for a roof over our head, for food, and for the four-year college education he was denied and which he was determined his children would have. He set aside money for those college educations, regularly. (I didn't appreciate it at the time.) He bought a car, a Pontiac, the greatest car in the world, he thought, which he and no one else would drive. He would also continue, to my mother's great chagrin, to give money to Nonno Sammie and Nonna Sara. There was nothing left over for extras. And he spent Friday and Saturday nights away from home, playing poker at the local Moose Club. My mother rebelled.

Mom was determined her children would have books and go to movies and participate in various sorts of lessons and activities. Since my father would not provide them, she took what seem to me heroic steps for those days. First, she learned to drive. Then she took a position as night nurse in a local hospital, eleven p.m. to seven a.m., working while we slept. With her earnings she bought a used car, a black and white Dodge with massive tail fins. Now she had freedom, her own income, and a kick-ass vehicle

Mom was determined her children would have books and go to movies and participate in various sorts of lessons and activities.

that out-gaudied my father's. The Dodge became my mother's "room of her own." She could be independent, and buy all the things she wished her children to have—encyclopedias, dance and piano and swim lessons and Little League games, movie tickets and weekly trips to the public library.

Her first effort that survives in my memory was to enroll me in dance class. I am not now, nor have ever been, a particularly graceful person that I can tell. But my teacher "saw something." The television station in the nearest large town of Bluefield hosted a weekly talent show, the "Hotpoint Varieties", named after a brand of appliance. It was the sort of thing local television stations did back in the 1950s. Every week, three contestants competed live, and the audience voted by telephone. I recall the heat of the lights in the studio, the studio audience a distant rumbling creature. A classical pianist went first, a vocalist second. Then I came out in my red velvet costume that my mother had sewn, a perky sequined cap on my head, and sang a quick song that started, "My momma says that I am just a scalawag." I don't recall the next verses, but the last line was "And this is how I go do town." I proceeded to do my tap dance routine, twirling my arms and smiling the whole time. Needless to say, I won. How could the audience, sitting in their homes in the coal camps of McDowell and Mercer Counties, vote against the cute little girl from Black Wolf in favor of the high-falutin' adults?

Fortunately, my mother was realistic, and indeed, even at that tender age, I was myself. I knew that, for talent, I couldn't touch the other two acts, who had entranced me as I watched them. I was not surprised, or hurt, when at the end of the year I did not make the finals in the competition. My mother had prepared me. But she gave me a sense that I could do anything I wanted to do, and do it in front of people, and I would be okay.

■ ■ ■

We paid a visit to Nonna Sara a year or so later. My mother was growing a garden, and in an attempt to keep the peace with her mother-in-law, had filled a paper grocery bag— what we called a "poke"—with freshly picked vegetables. My brother and I waited in the back seat of the car. I don't know what passed between the two women, but they argued. My mother ran back to her new car and began to drive away.

As my brother and I watched out the rearview window, my grandmother hurled the poke and its contents at the back of the car, scattering tomatoes and carrots in the coal dust. We escaped with wheels spinning like in the movies our mother paid for every Saturday matinee.

■ ■ ■

My father was not pleased, but my mother's rebellion was the price she exacted for staying with him. To his credit, he did not bully her into giving up her new independence. My father was not the bullying type. And I was grateful. My mother was providing me with the tools I would need to fulfill my special purpose. I didn't know quite what that was, but it involved large amounts of time to daydream and immerse myself in books. I avoided everyday chores as much as possible. My mother made a token effort to enlist me, but put up no resistance when I claimed incompetence. I could dust the furniture with lemon-scented polish well enough. For a while Mom asked me to wash dishes, which I hated because of the contact with floating globs of leftover food in the greasy water. My mom was a nurse, used to bodily fluids and effluvia. I was not, so I thought she should do the dishes. Most often I copped to drying the dishes because my mother, who was particular about dishwashing, didn't trust me. (In later years, after dishwashers were invented, she continued to wash her dishes in soap and water before placing them in the machine.) As for other household chores, I was semi-competent at vacuuming. My ironing and bed making did not meet my mother's standards—no sharp creases in trousers, no Army-tight corners in the days before fitted sheets. Likewise she disapproved my half-hearted (on purpose) swiping of the kitchen floor with a broom or mop. Most often I was relieved of duty so I was free to go off and read. My mother didn't chide me, and I sensed she was not unhappy to let me off the hook. She consulted with my teachers and let me know that, though I was "immature for age"; I was "very smart". I retreated to my library books, and my perusal of the new set of the *World Book Encyclopedia* my mom had purchased, which I read cover to cover, several times over.

I never consciously thought of writing in those days, although my mother claimed that as a small child I announced I wanted to be a "poemer." I don't recall that. I do know that I told stories in my head continually, during boring classes, during long car rides. But I never wrote them down. I knew I would not be good at it, because I was a hillbilly, and hillbillies, the TV told me, were ignoramuses who had no stories to tell that were of interest to anyone else. And I never, ever, wanted to waste my time doing something I wasn't good at.

As soon as I was able to read, my mother put the local newspapers in my hands, the morning *Bluefield Daily Telegraph* and evening *Welch Daily News*. My father read them first, but I was second in line. My mother subscribed to the *Reader's Digest*, which I consumed as diligently as I now do the *New Yorker*. We received no other magazines; in high school I was made to feel inferior by a fellow student because we did not subscribe to *Time*. I now consider that no great loss. The maudlin, right-wing sentimentality of *Reader's Digest* was enough of a distortion of reality, but it at least taught empathy of a sort. I was especially stricken by an account of a girl my age who died of leukemia, and wondered how I would have handled such a situation.

Unexpectedly, it was my father who opened up another vista. Every year, he and his *compares* gathered in New York City to watch the Yankees in the World Series. I assumed the Yankees always had a guaranteed spot in the World Series.

So my father would meet his fellow translators from the war. *Compare* Visco, originally from Chicago who had moved to Miami, and who we visited in our only trip to Florida. *Compare* Filetta, who settled in Virginia Beach and once brought his family to visit us in West Virginia. They gathered to watch the Yankees, Italy's team.

On his last trip to New York, my dad returned with a copy of *Charlotte's Web*, recommended by a bookstore clerk as a present for his little girl. Except for cheap Golden Books from Kroger, it was the first book I ever owned. All the real books I knew were locked in place at my grade school or the county library, prisoners allowed to escape now and then but forced to return. The concept of owning a book that you didn't have to return to the library was life-changing. *Charlotte's Web* was beautiful and I could keep it beside my bed and read it every night and never let it go. I could cry over it, and whisper to myself, *Some pig*. I adored *Charlotte's Web*, and was shocked my father had provided it. How on earth did he think to find a bookstore, a place so exotic I could not imagine it? Why did my father think it important to buy me a book? Such an anomaly causes me to question the narrative of my life that I constructed over the years. My father, who spent so much time away from us, who I was never close to, was more present than I knew. Or perhaps one of his Army buddies suggested the purchase. I would never know, for my father never explained anything. It fell into the category of things he was not able to talk about, perhaps because he lacked the English for interior thought.

■ ■ ■

When my mother began working the night shift, I suffered insomnia for a time, fretting because she was not in the house. I don't know if it was really insomnia. I would stare at the ceiling for what seemed like hours, unable to sleep, but suddenly it would be morning. I also wandered, bothering my father while he watched television. Jack Paar would be pontificating on the black and white screen, I would pester, and he would say go back to bed. I sometimes went to school exhausted. My mother took me to doctors, but nothing was diagnosed. After a time, I began to sleep again.

How did my mother manage those nighttime hours? She slept while my brother and I were at school. In the summer she used her income to buy us a membership at the Gary Country Club, a private swimming pool. By a stroke of luck, the pool was only half a mile from our house, so we could walk the railroad track and up the hill. We went every day in those summers, and I fell in love with swimming pools. My mother was afraid of water, for she had almost drowned as a child, trying to cross a swollen river on the back of a mule. But she trusted us to the lifeguards and fell asleep for hours while we cannonballed and performed flips from the diving board. We spent so much time in the pool we changed colors.

I used to stand before the mirror and study my naked summer body—my torso milk-white, my face and arms and legs dark chestnut-brown. As fall progressed, my parti-colors faded and I mourned the loss of the pool.

■ ■ ■

It was not just my mother's discomfort with animals in the house that made Socks an outdoor cat. We had not heard of litter pans, not in the West Virginia coalfields. Perhaps they were in use elsewhere, but I never saw one until I was a teenager and we had moved to the city. Cats must go outside to do their business, so they should stay outside.

My parents did the best they could by Socks. The tiny furnace room had a door that led outside so that my father could carry buckets of coal from the coalhouse to the furnace without tracking the dust into the main house. On the coldest nights, Socks was allowed to sleep inside the furnace room beside the warm stove. She also was allowed to have her kittens there, if we could catch her before the kittens were born.

My mom tried to keep up with the kitten bearing at first. She had a good sense of when Socks was filling out and acting strangely, and then the cat would be confined. But the pregnancies occurred several times a year. We did not think of spaying. Veterinarians performed that procedure, we had vaguely heard, but the nearest vet was an hour and a half away in another state, and likely expensive. It was, in fact, an odd concept—a doctor just for animals. As a health care professional, my mother found it puzzling. What sort of person would study long years, as she had, just to treat an animal?

So Socks had her litters, one after another. The first year my dad, ever with an eye to money like any child of the

It was, in fact, an odd concept—a doctor just for animals. As a health care professional, my mother found it puzzling. What sort of person would study long years, as she had, just to treat an animal?

Depression, sold the kittens for a dollar a piece. That didn't last. We next had to beg friends and neighbors to take the kittens. After a time, that also failed.

One of the early litters came to a bad end. Socks had been given a break from nursing to go outside to tend to business. And somehow, someone forgot to close the door to the furnace room. When my mom noticed and went to close it, she found Candy the dog inside with the kittens.

Mom tried to shield the contents of the box from me as she carried it out, but I slipped closer and saw. The tiny kitten heads had been removed neatly, one by one, and lay beside the torsos. Another reason to hate Candy.

This also seemed to break my parents' resolve to deal kindly with the kittens. Circumstances were getting away from them. My mother stopped noticing when Socks was due; Socks had her kittens elsewhere. Perhaps she went under our house, or a neighbor's. Perhaps she went to the basement of the now-abandoned company store, or to some lair on the mountainside. Wherever she went, she disappeared for days at a time, except to appear briefly for her supper. Finally she would return, and things would go back to normal. She never came back with kittens in tow. Perhaps predators more wild than Candy killed them, or they died of starvation, or went feral. I imagined tiny kitten skeletons scattered beneath the floorboards of our house.

■ ■ ■

Here is my strongest memory of my cat Socks. Except when she was gone with kittens, she came when I called. It didn't matter where she was. When I wanted to visit with her, I would stand on the back porch and call "Kiiiiity, kitty-kitty-kitty! Kitty Socks!" Sometimes I had to call three or four times, but after a moment she would come, a black form streaking down the mountainside path, or jumping through the broken window in the company store basement. I would hold her, stroke her. She would purr.

■ ■ ■

Because I was infatuated with kittens, I was allowed to choose one from an early litter, though my mother stipulated it be a tom, not another litter-bearer. I named the male kitten Junior. He looked very much like his mother, mostly black with white tips on his feet. But when he was a big kitten, a neighbor dog attacked him. The dog tore Junior's back leg nearly off, left it hanging by bloody threads of flesh attached to the white bone.

I wrote about this years later in my novel *The Unquiet Earth*. One character, Rachel, was partly inspired by my mother. She says, "I was a good nurse. I could diagnose as well as any doctor and I didn't panic in a crisis...I even did veterinary work, sewed the hind leg back on a black tomcat that had been caught by dogs. The leg was dangling by the bone but Hassel Day wrapped the cat's head and body in a thick towel and held it while I sewed with a plain needle and thread, careful to match the layers of fat and sinew, like piecing a quilt. Later the cat walked without a limp. I could have made a surgeon, if women had thought to do such things in my day."

Mom could have made a surgeon if she'd been encouraged. I witnessed the operation, can see her dipping the needle and thread into rubbing alcohol and stitching through pink flesh as methodically as though hemming one of the dresses she made for me, while Randy, a teenaged boy from the camp, held the poor kitten, out of its mind with pain and wrapped in a towel, in a tight vise. Junior grew up to walk without a limp, and he survives in a book.

■ ■ ■

Junior grew to be a big tom, and poor Socks continued to produce her litters, some of them likely provided by her own son. The years passed and a great change came. Our coal company began selling off its houses. Many miners were leaving as thousands of jobs disappeared. The coal companies decided to sell of their houses to unsuspecting residents who expected still to be kept on, as if the purchase of a house they'd never owned until now would secure their continued presence. In a neighboring coal camp several miles away, the doctor was let go, and moved to Lexington, Kentucky. His house, with ten rooms and attached office, was available for purchase. It stood on a street of other large houses built for professional employees, and the three-story brick superintendent's mansion stood at the end, surveying the company's domain. Because my father was a white-collar worker, an accountant who was assured he was safe, he decided to buy. Our tiny old house would finally be torn down as the company downsized.

My mother was thrilled to be out of the cramped wooden structure that had served several generations of miners. Now we would own our house on Company Row. We could fix it up any way we wanted. We would have a dining room. Four bedrooms. Playrooms in the old doctor's office. We would live on a paved street.

When the time came for our move, we threw Junior into the car. But Socks was nowhere to be seen. She'd been gone for days, tending another litter.

We left without her. I was eleven years old. I didn't know what to do. We'll come back, my mom and dad said. We'll look for her.

When we got to the new house, we threw open the car door. Junior bolted out. We never saw him again.

I know now. I know. You don't move an outside cat to a new location without enclosing him for a time, until he gets his bearings. You don't—

We didn't go back to look for Socks. I suppose we meant to, but just didn't get around to it. I suppose we thought if we found her, she would bolt as Junior had done. I suppose I was absorbed by the coming school year—seventh grade in a new junior high school, band, and boys. I suppose I meant to go back, but I was only a kid, I couldn't drive a car to go look for her, and after a while I forgot to ask my mom and dad.

■ ■ ■

I think about Socks often. I remember calling for her, and how she always came to me. Always. I see her, skinny and black, streaking down the mountainside toward home. I see her on the back porch, waiting for the door that never opens, the meal that never arrives. I wonder about forgiveness. ■

THE NIGHT EARTH STEPPED IN

That night when Earth stepped
between chasing moon and sun,
time shifted into slow motion
as we stood outside,
freezing cold,
to glimpse the rare transformation.
Its dramatic, ancient-sounding name
—super blood wolf moon—
caught our attention,
brought out something
from deep inside,
a hungering
that made us wait for darkness,
wait for a moment of magic
in the middle of the night.

We stopped our chatter to look.
The landscape gleamed,
awash in moonshine
on fresh snow.
At last our screen-deadened
eyes adjusted and allowed
the world to come into focus,
not just the red moon
framed by naked tree limbs
but the full picture,
the sharp scatter of stars
glittering
against blue-black sky,
waiting for us to see,
waiting for us to howl.

JAYNE MOORE WALDROP

THE YEAR WE FELL APART

We'd been to more doctor visits
than movies or dinners or walks
in the woods. The kitchen island
became a pharmacy counter
cluttered with bottles and lists
and receipts left in clear view
lest we forget the next dose to kill
our pain or keep our blood
from throwing clots or our bones
from crumbling like dust to dust.

A new walker sits parked beside
a straight-backed chair, required
accessories in this post-op world.
The equipment reminds us
of our parents, the late-in-life
assisted-living version we've tried
to erase, the ones we said we'd
never be like. Surely the walker
isn't for either of us, in our minds
still way too young and strong.
When pain comes round like hands
on a clock marking time, we hear
their voices: *Stand up straight.*
Your body is a temple. If you don't
have your health, you have nothing.

For a moment we feel young again,
transformed into pissed-off
teenagers needing to sulk
and blame someone, to scream

I hate you to our weak, broken parts.
We want to slam doors, cuss,
turn up the music, and lay rubber
as we escape this place.
Was the year we fell apart
programmed into our genes
as beyond-the-grave punishment
for not minding them, or did our
choices chisel this reality into stone?
Wonder if we get a chance
to grow up before we grow old.

JAYNE MOORE WALDROP

NEAR EL PASO ON THE FEAST OF THE HOLY INNOCENTS

Herod was furious when he realized that the wise men had outwitted him. He sent soldiers to kill all the boys in and around Bethlehem who were two years old and under....A cry was heard...weeping and great mourning. Rachel weeps for her children, refusing to be comforted, for they are dead.
                                                                    —Matthew 2:16-18

Word came on December 28th,
the Feast of the Holy Innocents,
the day set aside to remember
children massacred

> by a ruler who called himself great
> who feared a brown-eyed baby
> would cost him his throne.
> He ordered them killed,
> without exception,
> all the little boys of Bethlehem.

Word came on December 28th,
the Feast of the Holy Innocents,
not glad tidings, only news
of a dead brown-eyed boy,

> age eight, tracked down
> with his family, detained
> in the desert near El Paso.
> His cellmates watched as he grew
> weaker, as his skin flamed hotter
> his eyes glossed brighter.

The boy showed signs
of the flu, signs left
untreated, untranslated
by those executing orders

of a ruler who calls himself great.
Word came on December 28th,
the Feast of the Holy Innocents.
Weep for her children.
Refuse to be comforted,
for they are dead.

JAYNE MOORE WALDROP

BOOK REVIEWS

Karen Salyer McElmurray. *Wanting Radiance.* **Lexington, Ky.: University Press of Kentucky, 2020. 272 pages. Hardcover. $24.95.**

Reviewed by Julie Hagy

The open palm on the cover of Karen Salyer McElmurray's third novel, *Wanting Radiance*, draws my daughter's attention. Across the illustrated hand, lifelines and map lines are etched. My daughter's five year old fingers, after pulling out my bookmark, trace the lines down the fingertips. "Where do these lines go to?" she wants to know.

Meet Miracelle Loving, fortune teller. Miracelle is a second-generation drifter and card reader. She's an expert at reading maps, tracing roads that keep her drifting from place to place. She also dabbles in fortune-telling.

When Miracelle was a child, her mother, Ruby, was murdered during a fortune-telling session. Miraclle never knew the killer or the circumstances around the murder. Now, as a thirtysomething, Miracelle is stuck in a pattern of loveless encounters, in odd jobs, in the restless cycle of moving from place to place. Stuck looking for love and purpose.

Miracelle thirsts for love but feels constricted and burdened by her unresolved past. She doesn't know her father. She doesn't know the motivation or the individual behind her mother's murder. Guided by Ruby's spirit, Miracelle goes on a quest to find her father, tracing the past, and learning about her roots along the way.

Wanting Radiance is deeply rooted in character, place, and the abnormal. The characters who populate, and sometimes haunt, the pages of *Wanting Radiance* are a ragtag, original bunch, unlike any other assembly you'll find in literature. Take for instance Ruby, Miracelle's mother. In life, Ruby, prophetess and fortune teller, makes potions out of plants and bones and scares people with her prophecies. In death, she whispers guidance in her daughter's ear. Cody Black, a handsome, tattooed man, walks the streets of Knoxville with Miracelle, introducing her to Willy's Wonderama, a museum of strange phenomena, and also to the idea of staying in one place. Della, who hires Miracelle under the table at the Black Cat diner, is a rough, capable woman. She's just as expert in the kitchen as she is fixing carburetors in her garage out back. Tragic Russell Wallen buys up the land, coal, paper and timber, but he ends up owning next to nothing to show for it. Then, there's drifting Miracelle, washing her underwear out in her motel sink. McElmurray does not spare her characters flaws, yet she manages to make them heartbreakingly relatable. Despite or perhaps because of their flaws, these characters help orient each other, finding their ways towards healing, love, and home.

The settings in McElmurray's novel are as unique as the characters. I felt uncomfortable at times in these new terrains:

a haunted room, a strange church gathering in the woods, a Texaco turned tattoo parlor, examining human oddities in a museum. The turns, the people, and the places are anything but predictable.

The novel is a journey, representative of both the literal and figurative wonderings of the protagonist. "Do wounds grow inside us from so far back we can never know the beginning of that hurt?" McElmurray asks. As the characters grapple with this question, a clear endpoint grounds the novel: the quest for love. Miracelle takes a strange, healing journey there.

In *Wanting Radiance*, McElmurray allows the reader to enter a world foreign to many of us. It's a world where potions burble, ghosts whisper, fortunes are told, human oddities are catalogued. It's a world where tarot cards are read, fiddles tuned, Bibles passed; where news clippings discovered in the basement of a museum of oddities points a young woman towards a hidden past. It's a world where love and healing are sought. It's a world where religion and witchcraft, real and mystical collide. It's just familiar enough to make the strange seem possible.

Part love story, part mystery, part ghost story, *Wanting Radiance* is told from the perspective of multiple characters, across the span of decades. The weaving between perspective, time, and place creates a generational narrative of longing, hurt, and quest for love.

My daughter's fingertip follows a palm line on the book jacket from wrist to fingertip. "You can pick a road," she informs me. I join her on the impromptu terrain, tracing lines across the palm. She assigns names to different regions of the palm, then her finger zooms off. "I'll meet you back home," she says, succinctly capturing of the essence of *Wanting Radiance* unaware.

Ashley Blooms. *Every Bone a Prayer*. Naperville, Ill.:
Sourcebooks Landmark, 2020. 352 pages. Softcover. $16.99.

Reviewed by Hannah D. Markley

"Dear Reader," Ashley Blooms
writes in a preface to her debut novel,
"I wrote this book because I wanted
(and needed) to explore the ways that
trauma impacts individual, familial,
and community identity...[and] how
we find a way back to each other
and to ourselves." Her letter makes
a promise for *Every Bone a Prayer*:
that the book will be a prescient
exploration for this time when societal
and individual trauma have dominated conversations and
many lives. From the first page, Blooms establishes herself
as a thoughtful and careful detailer of the traumatic content.
She says, dear reader, the story ahead will be difficult. Yet
with a clear, forward communication of its heavy content,
she ensures the characters and the reader are not alone in
the trauma, that she herself can be trusted through whatever
comes and however it ends.

True to her word, the reader feels the bodily and
generational trauma in the descriptions and through the
perspective and imagination of the central character. Misty
is introduced as a child living with her father, mother, and
sister, but quickly the reader sees the tension in the marriage
and simultaneously, with Misty and her older sister, Penny. As
Misty and Penny tussle on one side of the trailer, her parents
throw verbal jabs on the other. She feels the discord between

her parents, hears ominous proclamations from her father and watches him leave. After the opening scene of conflict, a tearful Misty scrambles down to the creek near the house. There she comes alive—or rather, everything else comes alive around her. Misty describes her mother teaching her how to pray:

> *"Now open up your heart. It's more listening than saying anything, but you can ask for things, too. You open up and wait for God to speak to you"...[Misty] listened for God—her chest a door flung wide open; her heart the golden light spilling onto the floor, eating the darkness whole. She invited everything inside.*

Instead of prayer becoming a way to talk to God, learning to pray catapults Misty into a mystical journey of opening herself to the world. Nature becomes her confidante and teacher.

Blooms lyrically describes Misty's connection to the animals, trees, creek, and even to her family's trailer, but it is the crawdads that become Misty's particular friends. As she listens to the nonhuman world, Misty learns that everything has a name, and those names communicate the essence of each being, human or nonhuman. The prose pulls the reader into Misty's connection to the world through vividly captured textures and sounds, most often through the lens of her body. In a scene describing a forest, Blooms writes, "The trees filled Misty to the brim with wonder and a sense of unquestioned belonging. A rootedness so deep that she was surprised to find her legs could bend when she opened her eyes."

The world-building in the novel seems rushed. Misty's connection to nature is evident from the first few pages, but her communications with the crawdads and other nonhuman beings lapses into descriptive paragraphs detailing feelings and experiences rather than launching the reader into a vivid scene where, as the observer, one can enter into the communication, not just feel a vague sense of connection. The reader's distance from Misty's perspective is exacerbated by general descriptions of the natural world and animals. This trend is also true of characters. For example, William, a neighbor, is introduced early in the novel and briefly described as a peer and a best friend-type to Misty. Their interactions move quickly into a more complicated relationship without bolstering up the initial claim of friendship. In the beginning, in particular, his character appears flat compared to Misty. Overall, the scenes and characters are not always as alive or textured in the ways Misty seemed to be living them. However, the scenes and characters do gather depth as the narrative develops.

What Blooms does with arrow-like accuracy is to describe how trauma exists in the body—how it feels and how it settles in the mind and in the imagination. Using fragmented memories and clipped images, the reader is vaulted into the emotional stream of Misty's traumatic flashbacks, and into the inevitable disconnection and battle to stay present to the world and a body after trauma.

Every Bone a Prayer fuses perceived reality with the mystical and invites the reader into the truest of worlds, a world where choices and traumas affect the deepest parts of one's name. The science-fiction-like blur between what is real and not real in Misty's life accurately mirrors trauma and its aftermath, where a victim sifts through what is true about themselves and their experience. With courage, deep understanding, and kindness, Blooms takes on a challenging task with self-awareness and grace, inviting readers into the arduous, uncertain journey of staying connected to a place, to loved ones, and to one's truest self, even when the easiest path forward is to forget.

Jessica Cory, ed. *Mountains Piled Upon Mountains: Appalachian Nature Writing in the Anthropocene.* Morgantown, W.Va.: West Virginia University Press, 2019. 360 pages. Softcover. $27.99.

Reviewed by Emily Masters

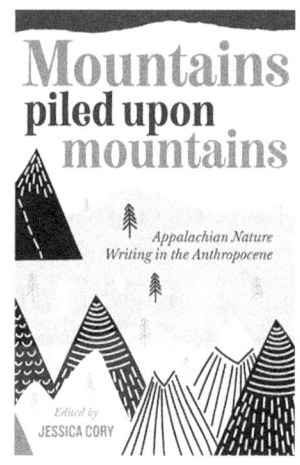

Geometric lines of peaked mountains designed by artist Than Saffel rise on the cover of Jessica Cory's edited collection *Mountains Piled Upon Mountains: Appalachian Nature Writing in the Anthropocene*, while coal mining equipment shaves the top off of another mountain in the background. The collection is timely to say the least. As the world shelters in place, holding its breath while Covid-19 sweeps the earth, people are beginning, slowly, to turn back to nature and what it has to offer. At the same time, climate change and human activities are rapidly shifting the natural world as we know it. This anthology calls to attention the variety of ways in which humans interact with nature, both the benefits and consequences of this interaction. In Cory's own words, "[T]his collection represents a wide swath of Appalachian engagement with nature during a time of great environmental change." Our environment is changing faster than we can keep tabs on, every discovery finding further loss—of life, of ice, of biodiversity, of temperature consistency, of mountains.

Mountains Piled Upon Mountains includes writing by beloved Appalachian authors like Ann Pancake in her "Letter to West Virginia, November 2016," alongside poems, essays, and short stories from both familiar and lesser-known writers in the region. The collection is split into seven sections, each focusing on a different aspect of human relationships to nature in Appalachia: Contemplate, Recount, Destroy, Preserve, Protect, Evolve, and Celebrate. These themes will be familiar to anyone who has experienced the complex relationships people in the region have to the natural world. In fact, it is difficult at times to recognize which section one is in because so many of the themes overlap.

In her introduction, Cory says, "The internal dialogue that the natural world facilitates can be pivotal not only to writers but also to the rest of us as we struggle to fit in moments of self-reflection amid our busy schedules and demanding societal pace." Cory does a good job confronting the complexities of Appalachia's struggling relationship to the natural world, allowing space in this collection for everything from coal mining and shifting biodiversity to appreciation for the sheer amount of beauty ready to be discovered in the Appalachian Mountains if one only takes the time to look. The writers included in the collection are certainly looking. To write about nature, one must spend time in it, watching, listening, observing, and the nature writing in the collection is vivid in its descriptions of mountains, water sources, forests, and the species within.

Many of the stories and poetry in the collection are lovely, but the essays Cory has selected stand out as particularly powerful and empowering. Heather Ransom's "Stockholm State: A History" examines the ways in which those living and working in Appalachia are committed to the very systems that keep them and the environment down. Laura Henry-Stone's

"Hemlocks, Adelgids, and People: Ecological Learning from an Appalachian Triad" takes a look at how three species interact in ways that can harm the overall ecology of a place. Jim Minick's "How to Avoid the Widow Maker" teaches about the difficulties, dangers, and rewards of working to maintain a healthy forest brandished only with chainsaws and water. All of the essays, poems, and stories share a deep respect of and rootedness in the Appalachian region.

While I appreciated the way the writers call to attention such pressing environmental issues in *Mountains Piled Upon Mountains*, I wanted more. More passion, more consistency within the sections, more selections from more writers. Some writers are published in multiple sections, and while their writing is beautiful, I wanted a wider opening for exploration, exhibited in a wider range of writers in the region taking on questions about human relationships to nature. There are so many writers in Appalachia who write with an environmental bent, and I felt some of that was missing. That being said, the writing within stands as a powerful call to action.

"Perhaps changing the mind of a single reader is all it will take to change the larger man-versus-nature narrative," Cory writes. The poems, stories, and essays are compelling and rise to the challenge of asking readers to consider the natural world and their relationships to it with greater complexity and care. Readers should take time to sink into some of the beautiful writing *Mountains Piled Upon Mountains* has to offer and then go outside, immerse themselves in nature, and take time to think and appreciate and absorb. Take this collection as the call to action it offers: to preserve, to question, and to appreciate nature before it is too late. ■

PROPHECY

I quit smoking some time ago, and I do not miss the stench,
Nor the half-caught breaths, the wheeze of undiscovered asthma.
Rather, I miss the fire of it, drifts of smoke like incense,
The seeking of ways, a step outside to test the winds,
The slowing of time, the pull to a bare hilltop.
The red ember a divining rod to stir,
Pull the entrails of life all apart,
See the pattern and pray for guidance.
I was a prophet, then, a truth-seeker,
And no one came near who could not bear the weight of ashes,
The stench of death surrounding me.
Now, when I need to throw the bones, I step outside,
But what shall I find to cry to those who pass "Hold! Have you seen?"
How else can I carry a censor out into these holy streets?

AMY McCLEESE NICHOLS

HOLDING A TRILOBITE FOSSIL

On one end, you're chipped.
I can see how deep your shape
is laid. Geometric, you are
semi-circles stacked like cones.
You are tunnel's top, a long set
of tubes, time travel in my hand.
If I lick you, will your death
grow in me?

I wonder what will be left
of me, footprint or spine. Covered
in Earth layer, too, dug out.
What will I be called? Will
someone store this part of me
on their desk, rub me when
sad? Create a whole life
from my fragments,
grouting those extra spaces,
brushing bits away?

I want to make a ring setting
for you, torch the silver until it turns
orange, bend pliable metal around you.
I'd solder that outline to another piece
cut with a jeweler's saw. I'd put you
in your cradle gently, curling
the edges up over you to tuck you
in a forever bed.

I want to wear you, so I can touch you
anytime I want. I want people

to see you, the shape of you,
ask *What is that stone?*
A fossil, I'll say. Look at those
ghost grays. I carry millions of years,
a body once crawled on ocean's floor.
Extinct. Peer into it—you'll see
the future, too. Tell me. Is the world
kind to you?

JAMEY TEMPLE

2020 IN HINDSIGHT

Do you think we should buy a gun,
he asks on the way to the heart specialist.
The world seems crazy.

Married for 18 years, never owning
a gun or worrying about our safety
in rural Kentucky, I should be

startled, but shrug, unsure. You know
something is coming as if you've pressed
your ear to earth for confirmation—

hearing and feeling an approaching train,
its rumble. You can't get back up. It's coming
for you. You know it.

We've sheltered in place for most
of the year, only leaving for essentials
and doctors' appointments,

like living in a basement
just in case a tornado touches
ground overhead—you don't know

when it'll swirl and infect you with
fear from its howl, so you wait
and wait for the warning to expire.

What storm cell will strike—
viral or civil unrest? What history
are we repeating?

What about installing a security system,
he asks later. *It's expensive*
but you never know.

JAMEY TEMPLE

HOW TO MAKE LOSS REAL

Picture someone you love. Maybe your wife,
the way she smells when she steps out
of the shower, her hair dripping. Imagine
her scrunching those strands with a towel,
then rubbing lotion onto her thirsty limbs.
See her wrapping that towel around her, tucking
the ends into the towel dress below her armpit.
Watch her as she blows her hot breath on the fogged
mirror, wiping so she can see a Monet of herself.

That wife that you loved so well, the wife
that you held on cold nights when the kids
were tucked into warm beds, the wife you watched
fall asleep time and time again, what if
her breath is hot with fever? What if
she has a cough, so you take her to a hospital
where you can't go with her?

You hug her as you stand at the entrance,
watch as she walks through automatic doors. *I'll see you soon,* you say.
You don't know what to do when those doors close,
so you go back to the family van, staring for a few hours
at a building that has her in it, somewhere.

A nurse calls each day after the doctor's morning
rounds to give you updates. On day ten, she tells you
that treatment isn't working. *It's not looking good,* she says.
Would you like to say anything to her? I can hold the phone up to her ear.

You want to talk to your wife as if no one else is listening, but you don't
know if she can hear you, but damn it, you have to say goodbye.
You have to fit in everything you've never told her but should have.
You hear the machines beep as you say, *I love you*. You want to say
more. The words are in your head, but they can't push through.
You'll be mad at yourself years beyond this moment because you didn't
do more or say more. You'll wonder if she recognized your voice, if yours
was the last she ever heard through drug-induced sleep.

Your story will spread for a few days. *Look*
it can happen, it did happen to someone I know.
People will send you texts and cards—all of your boxes
will be full, but very few of those people will stand
next to you by your wife's closed casket.

After a few weeks, people will tire of your story.
You'll become the reminder of their worst nightmare,
so it's easier to forget you, to explain away all the reasons
why

As much as they tire of your story, you'll tire
of *I'm sorry for your loss* and *What can I do*

They turn away when you say

This is how we can join hands again, drink air.
This is how you save yourself, this
is how you don't become me.

JAMEY TEMPLE

CONTRIBUTORS

Cynthia Alby is a professor at Georgia College who is devoted to supporting others as they discover the power of teaching as a transformative activity. She writes and creates art on a farm called "Shangri-Baa" where she and her husband raise an endangered breed of sheep and share their home with a crew of rescued dogs.

Mallory Cash is an editorial and portrait photographer based in Wilmington, North Carolina. Her work has appeared in the Knoxville Museum of Art, *The Bitter Southerner, Salt Magazine, Dear Photographer Magazine, The New York Times, Encore Magazine, O'Henry Magazine, Garden and Gun, Our State, PineStraw Magazine, Bold Life*, and has been featured in galleries in Tennessee, Virginia, and West Virginia.

Wiley Cash is the *New York Times* bestselling author of the novels *The Last Ballad, A Land More Kind than Home,* and *This Dark Road to Mercy*. The founder of the Open Canon Book Club and co-founder of the Land More Kind Appalachian Artists Residency, he has been a fellow at the MacDowell Colony, Yaddo, and the Weymouth Center. He serves as the writer-in-residence at the University of North Carolina-Asheville and lives in North Carolina with his wife, photographer Mallory Cash, and their two daughters.

Barbara Costas-Biggs is a poet and librarian from Appalachian Southern Ohio. Her work has appeared recently or are forthcoming from *Lost Balloon, Northern Appalachian Review, Mothers Always Write, Glass, Ghost City Press, 8Poems*, and others. Her poem "Naked in the Macy's Changing Room, Trying to Think About Anything Other Than the Election" won the *Split This Rock* Abortion Rights poetry contest in 2017. Her MFA is from Queens University of Charlotte, and her MLIS is from Kent State.

Victoria C. Flanagan is the author of *Glossary of Unsaid Terms,* winner of Beloit Poetry Journal's 2020 Chad Walsh Chapbook Prize. Flanagan's writing has also been awarded an Academy of American Poets Prize, the Emerging Poets Prize from Palette Poetry, and a

Sewanee Writers' Conference scholarship, among other honors. Their work has appeared in *The Adroit Journal, The Boiler, Verse Daily, New South, Blackbird*, and elsewhere. A poet and essayist raised in small-town North Carolina, they hold a dual-genre MFA in poetry and nonfiction from Virginia Commonwealth University, and are the 2020-21 Ronald Wallace Poetry Fellow at the Wisconsin Institute for Creative Writing.

Denise Giardina is one of Appalachia's most critically acclaimed writers. The author of the novels *Good King Harry, Storming Heaven, The Unquiet Earth, Saints and Villains*, and *Emily's Ghost*, her work has received a number of literary prizes. An ordained deacon in the Episcopal Church, Giardina is also a community activist and a former candidate for governor of West Virginia. She graduated from West Virginia Wesleyan College in 1973 and earned a Master's in Divinity from the Virginia Theological Seminary.

Julie Hagy is a journalist and writer, from Virginia. Her work has appeared in AAA travel publications, *Lookout Magazine, 5280, Blue Ridge Outdoors, San Diego Weekly Reader*, among others.

Marc Harshman's latest collection of poems is *Woman In Red Anorak*, which won the Blue Lynx Prize. His fourteenth children's book, *Fallingwater*, co-written with Anna Smucker, was published in 2017. His 2016 poetry collection, *Believe What You Can*, won the Weatherford Award from the Appalachian Studies Association. His work has been published in *The Chariton Review, Appalachian Heritage, Gargoyle*, and *Shenandoah*, and he was named the seventh poet laureate of West Virginia in 2012.

Marie Manilla is a West Virginia native and graduate of the Iowa Writers' Workshop. Her books include *Shrapnel, Still Life with Plums: Short Stories*, and *The Patron Saint of Ugly*, winner of the Weatherford Award. Her essays have appeared in *Still, Word Riot, Cossack Review*, and elsewhere. "Pyro" is from a memoir-in-progress.

Hannah D. Markley served as the 2019-2020 Hindman Settlement School Creative Writing Fellow. Currently, she is an MFA candidate in Creative Nonfiction at the Rainier Writing Workshop and lives in central Kentucky.

Emily Masters is a graduate of Berea College and serves as book reviews editor for *Appalachian Review*. She is from Monteagle, Tennessee, where she lives on a farm with her family. Her work has been published in *Still: The Journal* and *The Pikeville Review*.

Amy McCleese Nichols grew up in Flemingsburg, Kentucky, and remains invested in the places and experiences of her home region. She was the 2016 recipient of the University of Louisville Creative Writing Award for Poetry, and her work has also appeared previously in *Pine Mountain Sand and Gravel* and *Appalachian Review*. She holds a doctorate in Rhetoric and Composition from the University of Louisville and currently serves as the Director of Writing Resources at Berea College.

Dr. Sylvia Bailey Shurbutt serves as Professor of English at Shepherd University in Shepherdstown, West Virginia, where she directs the Center for Appalachian Studies and Communities. Shurbutt's primary teaching and scholarly interests are English pedagogy, nineteenth-century British literature, linguistics, and Women's and Appalachian studies. The Appalachian Heritage Writer-in-Residence Project Director, Shurbutt enjoys music, flowers, and travel.

Jamey Temple is a writer and professor who teaches English at University of the Cumberlands in Eastern Kentucky. Her poetry and prose have been included in several publications such as *Rattle, Literary Mama, Kentucky Monthly*, and *Still: The Journal*.

Jayne Moore Waldrop is the author of *Retracing My Steps*, which was a finalist in the 2018 New Women's Voices Chapbook Contest (Finishing Line Press 2019). Her work has appeared in *Appalachian Heritage, Still: The Journal, New Limestone Review, Minerva Rising, Deep South Magazine, Anthology of Appalachian Writers*, and other journals. *Drowned Town*, Waldrop's linked story collection, is forthcoming from the University Press of Kentucky. She lives in Lexington, Kentucky.

www.ingramcontent.com/pod-product-compliance
Lightning Source LLC
Chambersburg PA
CBHW070604180626
46817CB00005B/1988